The Response Revolution

The pursuit of excellence in
teaching and learning

ROBERT POWELL

Robert Powell Publications Ltd
MOTIVATE AND ENGAGE LEARNERS

Published by Robert Powell Publications Ltd
56 Stockton Lane
Stafford
UK
ST17 0JS

First published June 2011
© Robert Powell 2011

ISBN-13 978-1-901841-01-5
ISBN-10 1-901841-01-4

Editor: Pat Winfield, Bookworm Editorial Services
Designer: Neil Hawkins, ndesign
Cover design: Chrissi Major, Promethean

Printed and bound in Great Britain by Cambrian Printers, Wales

Contents

Acknowledgements

I owe a great debt to many people and organizations that have helped in the production of this first edition of *The Response Revolution*. ActivExpression has been available for a number of years, but the Self-Paced features are relatively new and still evolving. The impact that Self-Paced has made on the classrooms, however, is startling. It is changing the way teachers think and act about feedback and response, and as readers will see from the case studies, it is engaging students of all ages and abilities. I decided, therefore, to write and publish this book now in order that others might share in the excitement of the pioneering teachers and students lucky enough to have experienced this technology in action.

The book has been written and published in a relatively short timescale, and as such will have its imperfections. Those imperfections can be laid entirely at my door and not at the door of any of the support teams or contributors who have made this book possible. Thanks must go firstly to Promethean and its wonderful team of professionals. No one individual can be named because so many people gave time from their busy schedules to help me. The kindness and generosity shown was remarkable and seems to be ingrained throughout the company.

In researching this book I have met, observed, and talked to teachers and students across the USA and the UK and have found them united in their passion for ActivExpression and the impact it has on motivation, participation, and progress in learning. Committed teachers also share another pressure—too much to do and not enough time! Despite this, all the contributors put in a great deal of time and effort so that readers might benefit from their passion and inspiration. I cannot praise them enough.

The United Church Schools Trust uses ActivExpression in all its schools in the UK, and Geoff Gould and Dan Bunker from its E-Learning team have been enormously helpful in allowing me to use or adapt flipcharts from the excellent training materials they have developed to support their schools in the use of ActivExpression. I am eternally grateful to the Trust and to Geoff and Dan for this invaluable support.

LEB Partnership is the leading provider of ActivExpression in the UK, with their success built upon their personal customer service and the team's willingness to demonstrate the technology in action in customers' own classrooms before a purchase is even made. The LEB team now has vast experience of ActivExpression in action, and they have not only provided me with valuable advice and ideas for the book but have contributed extensively to the "Tips for teachers" section. My thanks go to the whole team.

All authors need good Editors and Designers, and I have the best. Pat Winfield, the Editor, has the patience of Job to go with her technical skills and eye for detail. I cannot imagine completing a book without her. Neil Hawkins, the Designer, has coped with the huge challenge of meeting the author's vision, even though it changes by the hour, and he always meets the challenges I set him. My grateful thanks go to both Pat and Neil.

Finally I must offer special thanks to Tony Cann. Tony was the founder of Promethean and the inspiration behind ActivExpression, Self-Paced Learning, and this book. Despite having founded the world's leading developer of response technology, he knew it could be taken further. He saw the potential of a response system that went beyond the 'clicker' and ActivExpression and then Self-Paced learning was born.

Foreword

The experience of being in a classroom using an advanced learner response system is exhilarating. Suddenly all the students are engrossed. Silence dominates as every single learner participates with enthusiasm and intensity, as question after question appears on the handset screen with less than a second between them. The teacher follows the progress of each student on their computer screen, instantly identifying who is struggling and why. Intervention is in real time. In the meantime, if students get an answer wrong, they get a message sent immediately to their handset screens, enabling them to work out the error and correct it or ask for help.

Furthermore, those that get the answers right are automatically moved on to more difficult questions. So, we have differentiated teaching coupled with personalized intervention, with all students working on tasks at appropriate levels of challenge. At the end of the sessions, the teachers have no marking and the results can be stored for more detailed analysis at a later stage.

As we watched lessons where ActivExpression was being used, we realized that these devices were not just useful for assessments but could be at the very heart of learning; helping students and teachers, improving outcomes, increasing participation, and maintaining discipline. As well as improving learning, with teachers able to monitor progress, the efficient use of time will also provide more opportunities for them to engage in dialogue with students, strengthening relationships.

We must not forget that in addition to the learning benefits, ActivExpression will also save costs. Suddenly, technology is available for the same daily cost as a few photocopied worksheets, or the annual cost of a modest textbook; technology that will cost a fraction of a percentage of a day's schooling but will improve the education of every child and benefit the daily life of teachers.

I felt that this experience needed to be shared so I was delighted when Robert Powell decided to record in a book the real experiences of teachers who are leading this revolution in order to help others who want to join it. The first version of what will be an annual handbook will be far from perfect as we set ourselves a very short timescale for publication, but we hope it will confirm the amazing potential of ActivExpression to existing practitioners and inspire others to look more closely at this ground-breaking, learning technology.

Tony Cann
Founder Prometheanworld

Introduction: the search for excellence

Shared vision

Readers of this book expecting to find another technical manual full of jargon, understood only by those whose lives revolve around gadgetry, will be disappointed. This is not a book for "Techies," but a book for those who are passionate about Learning and Teaching, for those who strive to change the lives of learners in and out of the classroom, and for those who, in the pursuit of excellence, constantly seek new ways to motivate, engage, and inspire learners, creating access, success, and challenge in equal measure. These goals are universal. While countries may disagree on political, economic, and social issues, in education there is a shared vision due to the accepted link between education, economic development, and social mobility: raising levels of educational achievement is an aspiration for governments, industry, those in public life or service, parents, and students.

There is no consensus, of course, on how best to raise educational standards. Political, social, religious, and cultural influences have a huge impact upon policies at government, regional, and district level, and no country yet has been able successfully to break the link between poverty and low educational attainment.

The question of "how" best to raise achievement has been the subject of education research all over the world; Professor Dylan Wiliam has reviewed the evidence and has clear views on this issue. It is the quality of teaching that has the most impact:

> *In the classrooms of the best teachers, students learn at twice the rate they do in the classrooms of average teachers—they learn in six months what students taught by the average teachers take a year to learn. And in the classrooms of the least effective teachers, the same learning will take two years.* [1]

Wiliam argues that achievement and expectations have risen continuously over decades, and hundreds of initiatives to improve standards continue to bombard education all over the world. But teaching quality, he says, is more important in determining success than class size, how students are organized in classes (e.g. in all-ability classes or grouped by ability), and more important even than the type of school attended. He argues that this is the case even for schools in areas of disadvantage:

> *… in the classrooms of the most effective teachers, students from disadvantaged backgrounds learn just as much as those from advantaged backgrounds, and those with behavioural difficulties learn as much as those without.* [1]

It is clear, therefore, that those engaged in leading initiatives to improve educational achievement, whether at government, district, school, college, or classroom level, would do well to focus on the characteristics of outstanding teachers and outstanding lessons. Decision makers who understand the ingredients of outstanding lessons will be better placed to develop initiatives to widen such practice and thus meet the aspirations of all those involved, at whatever level.

What are the ingredients of outstanding lessons?

Most adults will look back on their time at school or college and be able to recall those teachers who made the biggest impact upon their education and, for many, upon their lives. They will also remember those teachers whose influence was minimal or even destructive. This will be true even for senior citizens looking back 60 years or more; such is the impact teaching can have on individuals.

What are these memorable teachers like? I was asked to lead a conference on outstanding teaching and learning in 2008 which was attended by both teachers and students. In one session, all 80 participants observed a "learning conversation" with seven 18-year-olds about to leave high school and embark on a university education. In the 30-minute "conversation" I asked the students to share with the audience what they thought were the qualities of outstanding teachers and outstanding lessons.

There was remarkable agreement on the characteristics they identified:

- Lessons vary; good teachers don't do the same thing every lesson.
- The teacher who is passionate about the topic makes us passionate.
- The best lessons are well structured with clear purpose.
- Good teachers make sure you are supported or challenged; they recognize that students all have different needs.
- The best teachers let you know constantly how you are progressing.
- Good teachers sometimes make lessons "fun."
- The best lessons are fast-moving, making you think.
- In the best lessons, everyone is involved; in the worst, most just sit there passively.
- After they have assessed your work, the best teachers tell you exactly what you have to do to improve next time.

These are the views of some of the consumers, but it is interesting that they are matched by the findings of numerous research studies from the academic world and from the reports of independent inspection services.

Learning response technology

Learning response technology has been used in classrooms now for over a decade. In the USA and the UK, these applications are variously described as "clickers" or "voting pads" and certainly these descriptions accurately reflect the function of the early technology in this field. Voting technology was well used in certain areas of the school and college curriculum, and was particularly useful in closed, multiple-choice tests, in seeking opinions, and in "are you clear" and "true or false" types of activity. However, the technology had little impact in large areas of the curriculum, particularly those that relied on literacy, vocabulary, thinking skills, or open-ended numeric or language responses. That has all changed with the latest generation of learning response systems, and the one with the most comprehensive array of applications is Promethean's ActivExpression.

ActivExpression learning response handsets have been designed to support teachers in the development of outstanding teaching and learning. They are much more than just "clickers." They continue to offer users a "voting" facility, but they provide a much wider range of functions that go to the very heart of effective practice. Indeed, in the research for this book I found ActivExpression being used in all subjects, with all ages, including parents and other adults, and in a wide range of teaching and learning contexts including:

- lesson starters
- assessment for learning
- consolidation
- summative assessment
- new learning

- problem solving
- skills' development
- games, e.g. mental Math
- research (classroom, library, field trips)
- parents and community liaison

I not only found ActivExpression being used in a wide variety of contexts, but also witnessed and found evidence for the incredible impact the technology has on teachers and learners, both in normal single-question mode and when being used in multi-question, Self-Paced mode where instructions or questions are sent to the handset screen and learners work at their own pace.

What is remarkable is that the response of teachers and students to the use of this technology mirrors many of the characteristics set out earlier to describe outstanding teachers and outstanding lessons. The concepts of passion, pace, participation, feedback, differentiation, and progress appeared in nearly all of the teacher and student evaluations and these included teachers of 4-year-olds through all phases to post-16 students and adults.

Passion: Teachers and students alike are unanimous in their praise for the technology. Its use has a huge impact upon the motivation of learners, engaging even those prone to disaffection or poor behavior. The intensity of the concentration on the faces of learners when in Self-Paced mode is amazing; the silence is eerie!

Pace: There is a noticeable increase in the pace of lessons when ActivExpression is in use. Few learners are off task even for a moment and in Self-Paced mode no learner has to wait while others complete a task. Some teachers even introduce a competitive element to the lesson, which further increases the focus and intensity of the learners. In the section of the book that examines the start of lessons, reference is made to the huge amounts of time lost waiting for lessons to start. Self-Paced activities transform this situation.

Participation: Experienced teachers will have come across a phenomenon that contradicts most of what we know about human maturity. One would expect that as learners grow older and more mature, they learn more, become more confident, and as a consequence participate more in discussion, debate, questioning, and other classroom activities. The opposite is true. Teachers who work with our youngest learners will confirm that 4-year-olds participate without fear. The words "I have a question" in such a class is greeted by a sea of hands and a chorus of "me, me" and they don't even know what the question is yet! Teachers of 13-year-olds upwards will often have no more than 3 or 4 "volunteers," the same learners each time; others, the "conscripts," only speak when asked a direct question. ActivExpression transforms such classrooms, enabling participation without fear, personal and private feedback, and providing even those who are shy and reticent with opportunities to contribute ideas, words, thoughts, numbers, or questions. Participation at 100% becomes the norm.

Feedback and decision making: Dylan Wiliam's research[1] suggests that the quicker the intervention, the more likely the student is to learn. He claims that summative assessment at the end of a topic or course has little impact upon learning, and even the normal assessment of learners' work through marking often takes place days or even weeks after the work has been completed and has little impact upon learning. ActivExpression provides instant feedback to both teachers and learners. Teachers are able to use the feedback to evaluate the teaching, recognizing instantly which areas of learning have been mastered and which need revisiting. They can also identify which learners need help on which questions and also those who now need to be challenged further. In some areas of work, these aims can be achieved instantly without the arduous and time-consuming marking and analysis. In Self-Paced mode, teachers can see when a mistake is made and intervene within seconds, ensuring that the same kind of mistake is avoided in subsequent questions.

Learners are also provided with instant feedback. Indeed, in the Self-Paced mode they can get a response after each completed question. In my research for the book, I was amazed at how many students actually welcome the feedback. Even a "sorry, incorrect answer" response on the handset was seen as helpful. As one student told me, *"if I know I have got it wrong, it helps me to put it right immediately."*

Differentiation: Successful teachers can raise the achievement of any group of students, not just those who are academically able. Such teachers recognize the importance of planning for differentiated learning opportunities. If tasks and activities are planned at one single level, there is a danger that those who quickly master the learning find themselves treading water, becoming bored while others catch up. On the other hand, students who find learning difficult struggle even to master the basics and soon become frustrated. Research studies in the USA and the UK have identified the dangers of such situations, with poor classroom behavior often resulting from the frustration caused by lack of differentiation in the planning of lessons.

ActivExpression in its Self-Paced mode has a unique approach to differentiation. Teachers are able to plan questions of different types, e.g. text responses, numeric responses, multiple choice, true/false, and rank in order. These questions can have varying degrees of challenge and learners receiving the questions on their own handset respond at their own pace. Successful answers can quickly result in those who are finding it easy facing increasingly difficult questions, while those who find the questions hard stay at that level until mastery takes place. Teachers or classroom assistants are able to conduct "live" monitoring of all individuals as their progress is recorded on the computer screen, allowing instant intervention when a problem is identified. ActivExpression replaces "teaching to the middle" with real and effective differentiation.

Progress reports: Many schools are "swimming" in data—administrators the world over are required to justify public investment in education by producing data that demonstrates progress for a wide range of indicators. Turning a mass of data into useful information that leads to better decision making is the key; the phrase "weighing pigs doesn't fatten them" is well known and makes a valid point. It is not data that improves learning but what you do with the information that data provides, and this is another context in which response technology excels. Earlier paragraphs pointed out how ActivExpression provides feedback in a busy classroom, providing teachers with the information that enables them to modify the lesson or intervene with individuals or groups—a process known widely as assessment for learning. The information on learning and progress can also be used for summative assessment because the data provided by ActivExpression can be produced in report form, saving teachers hours of work spent in marking, analyzing, recording, and reporting progress. The ActivExpression software will also allow teachers to export such data into the personal records of individual students, providing electronic academic profiles of their progress over time. Such summative data can be invaluable in decision making and will save teachers and administrators hours of time.

The Response Revolution

I began this introduction by stressing that this book was not a technical manual. I need to emphasize also that it not an academic study. It does not pretend to produce academic evidence that this technology is the best available. There may be existing systems that match the functionality of ActivExpression, but if so I have not seen them. Other products may emerge in time that will offer educators similar opportunities, but my focus in this book has been on a product that I have no doubt currently leads the world in response technology. The book's title reflects my views on the emergence of ActivExpression in the educational arena. I sincerely believe that it is the most significant development in education in the past 20 years and that it and similar systems will be the dominant technology for years to come. Its potential is enormous and the remainder of this book is devoted to demonstrating that to readers.

I have made huge claims in this introduction, but from now on I am going to let teachers and students take over. Many of the examples that follow are observations of real lessons, all of them used somewhere in the USA, UK, or elsewhere in the world. Some practitioners have contributed details of their lessons and these have been attributed. Readers will be able to see how ActivExpression opens the door to new and exciting vistas for those with a passion for teaching and learning. The only limits are those imposed by the imagination of the user. Read the comments of teachers and learners at the forefront of ActivExpression developments and you will begin to understand the excitement of those, like me, who are privileged to be involved with its evolving use in schools and colleges all over the world.

Robert Powell
June 2011

References
[1]   Wiliam, D. (2009). *Assessment for learning: why, what and how?* London: Institute of Education, University of London.

Assessment for Learning

Assessment in schools is a major industry in most countries. In the USA and the UK, for example, huge sums are spent from education budgets on one or more aspects of assessment. The amount of standardized testing in both the USA and the UK has grown over the past decades and it is easy to understand why. Spending on education is a priority in many countries and has shown a year-by-year growth in real terms in most industrialized countries.

Governments need to be accountable for this expenditure; investment in the police, therefore, should show a decrease in crime and investment in hospitals should see an improvement in health. In the same way, policy makers who increase spending on education want to justify the use of taxpayers' money by seeing raised levels of achievement in our schools. The easiest way to demonstrate this is through a program of local or national testing which produces data that can show the impact of the investment.

This testing agenda is now very important at school, district level, and state level, and in the USA and the UK league tables of school and local-area performance are now produced based on the data provided from such assessments. In England, inspection of schools is carried out by the Office for Standards in Education (Ofsted), and each inspection starts with an analysis of the data provided by the school before the visit. Most leadership teams in schools now have someone with expertise in data and many hours will be spent by them producing tables and graphs analyzing performance in a range of variables. The focus on testing has shown a natural growth in related industries. In both the USA and the UK, the biggest growth areas for publishers of educational resources are now testing and revision, in both book and digital formats. Sales of traditional textbooks are down. Major book stores now have whole sections with bookshelves stacked with "test-yourself" publications for home use as parents join the rush to ensure their children perform well in tests.

There are numerous studies both in the USA and in the UK which highlight the dangers of these high-stakes tests. "Teaching to the test," "narrowing the curriculum," "valuing what we test rather than testing what we value," "testing only those things that are easily measurable"—all of these criticisms have been leveled against policy makers relying on standardized tests. There is no doubt that such comments have led to an improvement in testing procedures. The redesign of such tests, however, is really a diversion from the key issue.

All such tests can be described as *summative*; they measure the performance of a learner, a cohort, a city, a district, or a country at a particular point in time. The data can be used to celebrate, to change, or to adapt policies, but there is very little evidence that summative assessment has any impact upon individual students. Indeed, there is growing evidence that an over-reliance on such tests can damage both the wider curriculum and the learning experiences of students. On the contrary, research across international boundaries, for example in the USA, in the UK, and in New Zealand, concludes that it is formative assessment that has the biggest impact upon students' learning.

Wiliam[1] points out that all the research findings on formative assessment suggest that it has a "consistent, substantial effect":

> ...whether the focus of the study is Portugal or the United States, whether it is looking at 4-year-olds or 24-year-olds, whether it is looking at music or mathematics, there appears to be these consistent, substantial effects.

Formative assessment is a key element of Assessment for Learning (AfL)—its purpose is to promote the learning, not measure it. Assessment that does not lead to action is not formative. Feedback is the process of communicating this information to teachers or learners.

Research in both the USA and the UK agrees on the importance of feedback in decision making. The most effective kind of feedback is **immediate**, not long term. For example:

- Feedback from questioning that shows the majority of students have not understood; the teacher now modifies the lesson to revisit this topic.
- Instant feedback to students that identifies mistakes. This feedback allows them to address the problems and make corrections before moving on. If early feedback had not been provided, they might have proceeded to compound the errors in subsequent work.
- Feedback from questioning that shows which individuals need further help or challenge; peer or teacher support is now offered.
- Feedback from peer assessment identifies an area of weakness; the student now redrafts the work.
- Feedback from self-assessment using the success criteria identifies an area for improvement; the student builds this into the next piece of work.

All of these examples are interventions that happen in a live classroom, not feedback given days or weeks after the event. As Wiliam1 points out:

> ...it is the shortest cycles of formative assessment – minute-to-minute and day-by-day – that have the greatest impact upon student achievement.

If the feedback from students informs the teacher that adjustments to the teaching are needed, and it is not done until the next lesson with that class:

> ...the teachers are already playing catch up... it is probably too late.[1]

So this clearly shows that schools seeking to improve levels of achievement will find it worthwhile to focus on strategies that improve the quality and range of immediate feedback, from teachers and from peers. Once schools identify that this is the most productive route to follow, the implications for classroom practice are clear; classroom organization, dialogue, participation, pace, and independent, paired, and group work will all need to be an integral part of lesson planning, and these issues are examined in more detail in the next chapter. Passive students and non-participation in questioning activities will result in minimal feedback, and if this happens opportunities for learning are lost.

Techniques for immediate feedback

There are a number of ways that outstanding teachers receive and encourage the use of feedback in their classroom, including these examples below.[2]

Questioning skills

The most obvious way of achieving immediate feedback is through skilled questioning. Outstanding teachers use the responses to gauge understanding, modifying the lesson plan when necessary.

Support groups

To get feedback teachers often say *"Are you all clear—any questions?"* There will be little response to this—owning up is potentially self-damaging ("put your hand up if you are stupid" is what the students think). Using peer "support groups" of three or four learners, where they discuss in the privacy and security of the small group things they are not sure of, can generate questions for clarification in less than two minutes.

Group questioning

Some teachers use techniques like *Question Time* or *Pass the Question*. These activities involve students in pairs or small groups preparing questions for their peers based on the lesson (or series of lessons). They are required not only to prepare questions but their own answers as well, evaluating answers when they come. In this activity, not only is the teacher getting feedback on understanding but peer assessment is taking place.

True/false

Another technique that combines pace, participation, and questioning is true/false using mini-whiteboards or electronic handsets. Teachers or students make a statement based on the learning from that lesson, e.g. *"saturated fat is found in butter."* Everyone has 10 seconds to record a true or false on their boards (or vote if using electronic response systems) and then the teacher calls "show me." Any misapprehension will immediately be evident.

Electronic feedback

Electronic, response technology, however, is the most effective way of ensuring that all students get instant feedback when they need it. Even the most skilled and committed of teachers will struggle to monitor the progress of all students, particularly in large classes of 30+ students. Promethean's ActivExpression handsets bring a completely new dimension to what is known as "live" feedback. The use of these handsets is the major focus for this book, but put simply, questions can be sent directly to the screen on the learners' handsets. As soon as they respond, another is sent, even if others have not answered—multi-question, Self-Paced learning, a phrase used over many generations as an aspiration, has now become a reality.

Furthermore, the software allows teachers to enter a message for each question to inform students if they are right or wrong; so messages such as "Well done, you are a math wiz" or "Sorry, have another go" can appear within a second of a learner answering a question. As one student in one of the case studies later remarked:

> *ActivExpression helps me to learn because I can find out right away if I got the right answer or not. I can also find out what I need to do to fix it.*

Another feature of ActivExpression is that difficulty levels can be increased in the programming so that, for example, every two correct answers results in a harder question next time. Within two minutes, some are on one difficulty level of question while others are on a wide range of other levels. This is an example of the feedback being used by the teacher to increase the challenge when learners are ready—very difficult to achieve in a large class with only the teacher's eyes to rely on.

Finally, the software has an amazing feedback for the teacher. While an assessment activity is being conducted, the live responses of all students are shown on the screen. Mistakes, long pauses, common errors, non-trying, or refusal to take part are all visible on the screen, allowing instant intervention. Furthermore, if teachers place their cursor over the question on the screen, it tells them exactly what students answered, allowing them to offer instant assistance. Live and immediate feedback is now a reality and this, as Wiliam pointed out, has *the greatest impact upon student achievement."*

References
[1] Wiliam, D. (2009). *Assessment for learning: why, what and how?* London: Institute of Education, University of London.

[2] These examples come from *Outstanding Teaching, Learning and Assessment: the handbook*. Robert Powell (2010). Robert Powell Publications Ltd. www.robertpowellpublications.com

Basic Functions of ActivExpression

ActivExpression is not just a "clicker" or voting pad. The new generation of response handsets still provides users with a voting facility, useful in many situations, but it now offers a wide range of functions that will allow more teachers to integrate the technology with their normal lessons to enhance the learning experiences of students.

This chapter is deigned for the new user or the educator interested in knowing more before investing in this technology, so it provides basic examples of ActivExpression in use, ones that a beginner could use without much preparation or training. More sophisticated and exciting examples follow in later chapters.

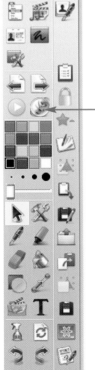

The response functions of ActivExpression are found on the Inspire tool below.

The ExpressPoll icon

The ExpressPoll menu

The ExpressPoll menu offers users the following functions:

- Multiple choice
- Rank in order
- Yes/No—True/False
- Likert scale
- Numeric response
- Free-text response

The following section will give examples of these in use in an imaginary Healthy Eating unit of work.

Multiple Choice

The multiple-choice options in ActivExpression are more sophisticated than those found in early response handsets, which only offer users one vote from up to six choices. ActivExpression gives users a much wider range of choices.

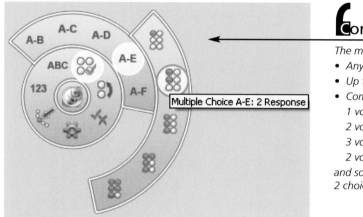

Multiple Choice A-E: 2 Response

Commentary

The multiple-choice wheel offers:
- *Any number of choices A–F*
- *Up to 5 choices in any vote*
- *Combinations such as:*
  1 vote from 6
  2 votes from 5
  3 votes from 4
  2 votes from 6
and so on. The one opposite has 2 choices from A–E.

Example

Context
The teacher is introducing the new topic to the class: Healthy Eating. She wants to know what the class thinks about healthy eating habits before the course starts so that she can assess (a) how much they already know and what their attitudes are at the beginning so that she can compare them at the end of the course; and (b) what kinds of challenge she faces in educating the class.

She has prepared a series of flipcharts for the unit of work and all students have ActivExpression handsets registered with their names. The first activity is an attitude assessment using multiple choice. The students are presented with the flipchart below which seeks to undertake a survey of current attitudes.

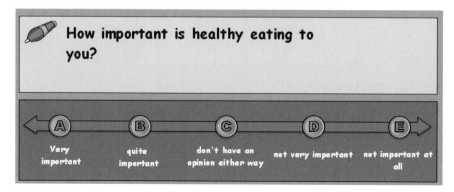

How important is healthy eating to you?

A	B	C	D	E
Very important	quite important	don't have an opinion either way	not very important	not important at all

All students have one vote from A "very important" to E "not important at all." As students vote, the teacher can see their names changing to yellow on the whiteboard.

The results are produced instantly and can be analyzed in a number of ways.

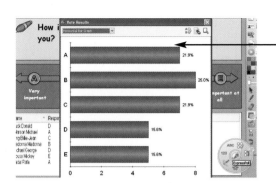

Commentary

This simple bar graph appears instantly the vote is complete and tells the teacher that there is a huge variation in the attitudes to healthy eating in her class, but that over 50% do not have a positive attitude to healthy eating. This table of results can be pasted to the screen if the teacher wants to keep it as a record.

Who answered what?
Another option for the teacher is to analyze how individual students voted. This information can be pasted and the image here shows the names of just a selection of the class and how they voted. (There is not enough space to include all the names but these are always provided.)

The teacher now asks the students to vote on the question below. This time they have a choice of **two votes** from a selection of **six**.

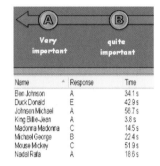

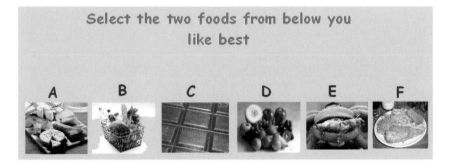

Once again the results are displayed instantly and she pastes to the screen to compare their attitude survey from before with their favorite foods now.

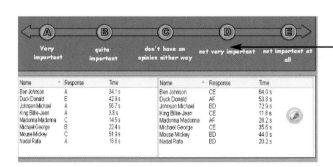

Commentary

The comparison is interesting. Ben Johnson selected "A" (healthy eating is very important) in the first vote, but chose chocolate and burgers as his two favorite foods! This kind of instant analysis helps the teacher to generate participation and discussion on the issues.

Yes/No—True/False

Yes/No—True/False—not sure

The Yes/No—True/False—not sure function in ActivExpression is one of the functions most likely to be used in a spontaneous, unplanned way in the classroom.

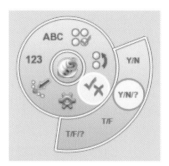

Teachers will often respond to contributions from students in class discussion with:

"Does anyone else agree with that?"

"I am not sure if you are right. What does anyone think?"

"Is that true?"

ActivExpression allows teachers to conduct instant polls when these occasions arise and use the results for further debate.

The teacher in the healthy eating lesson will have many occasions when this will happen, but has also planned a more formal use of the True/False poll.

Many students, and adults for that matter, have come to believe certain myths about diet, eating, exercise, and other health-related matters. The teacher decides to test the knowledge of the class with a True/False session.

4. Diet drinks don't damage your teeth

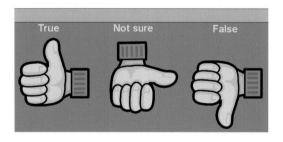

True   Not sure   False

The one on the left is no. 4. Other statements in the test:

1. Vegetarian diets are healthier.
2. Dairy products make you fat.
3. Vitamin supplements provide all the necessary nutrients.
5. Skipping meals is a good way to lose weight.

The results give the teacher instant feedback on the students' levels of understanding. This is more effective than asking them orally—most won't respond, others will just agree with their friends. With ActivExpression, however, there is no hiding place. The teacher achieves 100% participation and engagement, and the data provided is available to influence the rest of the lesson.

4. Diet drinks don't damage your teeth

True   Not sure   False

Name	Response	Time
Ben Johnson	False	27.3 s
Duck Donald	False	30.3 s
Johnson Michael	True	33.1 s
King Billie-Jean	False	17.2 s
Madonna Madonna	True	12.3 s
Michael George	True	24.5 s
Mouse Mickey	Don't Know	35.7 s
Nadal Rafa	Don't Know	22.3 s

Sort in order

The sort in order option in ActivExpression offers a facility where students are asked to sort or rank up to five items into an order of their choosing. So, it might be sort in order of chronology, order of importance, order of interest, order of like/dislike, and so on.

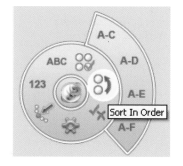

The teacher in this continuing example on healthy eating has produced the flipchart below showing the typical diet and life style of five characters: Wayne, Carrie, Josh, Kai, and Afa.

They have to work in small groups to rank their eating choices from "most healthy" to "least healthy."

The groups are told that they have to find reasons to justify their choices and that the results will be displayed for all to see.

Each group will use the sort function on ActivExpression when they reach agreement on the order.

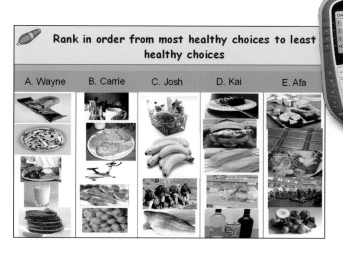

Once again, the results will be instantly produced and the teacher will be able to paste the results to the screen; then the real debate will begin.

Having the original choices on the screen alongside the pasted results will provide the class with wonderful feedback from the exercise, leading to heated debate as Rafa Nadal's team tries to convince George Michael's team that Josh is healthier than Afa.

Name	Response	Time
Ben Johnson	CBEAD	67.8 s
Duck Donald	ECBDA	82.8 s
King Billie-Jean	CEBDA	21.7 s
Madonna Madonna	CEBDA	34.4 s
Michael George	ECBAD	47.2 s
Nadal Rafa	CEABD	59.0 s

Likert

The Likert scale is used extensively by social scientists and market research analysts to undertake surveys of the public.

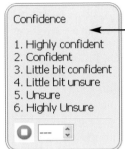

Confidence

1. Highly confident
2. Confident
3. Little bit confident
4. Little bit unsure
5. Unsure
6. Highly Unsure

Commentary

Typically, it is seen in the type of questionnaire that asks members of the public their views on an issue that is subject to debate.

The teacher in the healthy eating lesson decides to undertake a class survey on some of the ideas that are often presented in the media as a response to obesity and poor health related to diet.

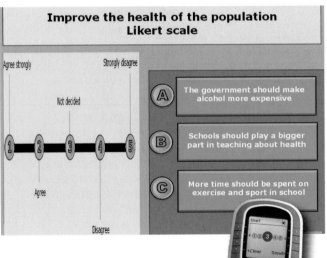

All students are invited to speak on each of these proposals and then the teacher asks them to use ActivExpression to vote on the 5-point scale from "Agree strongly" to "Strongly disagree."

As always, all the results are presented instantly and can be pasted to the screen.

These results can now be used in any follow-up work that the teacher decides upon. Indeed, this vote might have been undertaken before debating the issues, and small groups might then have worked collaboratively on each of the proposals, preparing arguments for and against. Another Likert vote would have seen if the persuasive powers or evidence presented by the groups had caused any changes of viewpoint.

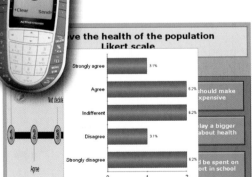

Numeric

ActivExpression offers users a numeric function where numbers can be entered.

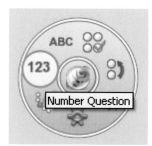

Once the numeric function is selected all entries on the keyboard will be numeric. Decimal points or commas can also be entered.

A new version of ActivExpression with a full numeric keyboard will be available later in 2011.

Two examples of the teacher in the healthy eating lesson using the number function are shown below.

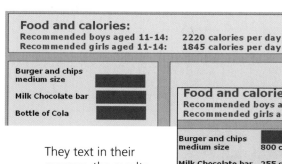

Food and calories:

Recommended boys aged 11-14:	2220 calories per day
Recommended girls aged 11-14:	1845 calories per day

Burger and chips medium size

Milk Chocolate bar

Bottle of Cola

In the first, the teacher asks students to guess how many calories are in three popular meals or snacks.

They text in their guesses, the results are displayed, and the answers revealed.

Food and calories:

Recommended boys aged 11-14:	2220 calories per day
Recommended girls aged 11-14:	1845 calories per day

Burger and chips medium size	800 calories
Milk Chocolate bar	255 calories
Bottle of Cola	240 calories

Name	Response	Time
Ben Johnson	180	51.9 s
Duck Donald	900	57.6 s
Johnson Michael	350	40.2 s
King Billie-Jean	400	29.9 s
Michael George	500	34.6 s
Mouse Mickey	675	46.1 s
Nadal Rafa	250	25.8 s

In this activity the teacher has listed a range of foods and put them randomly in one of two columns "healthy" and "not healthy."

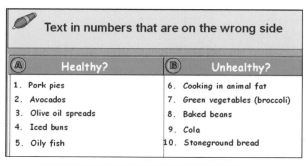

Text in numbers that are on the wrong side

Ⓐ Healthy?	Ⓑ Unhealthy?
1. Pork pies	6. Cooking in animal fat
2. Avocados	7. Green vegetables (broccoli)
3. Olive oil spreads	8. Baked beans
4. Iced buns	9. Cola
5. Oily fish	10. Stoneground bread

Each type of food is numbered. It is very simple—text in numbers, with a comma after each, that are in the wrong column.

Name	Response	Time
Ben Johnson	1579	168.0 s
Duck Donald	1569	161.0 s
Johnson Michael	34510	119.6 s
King Billie-Jean	45710	86.2 s
Michael George	1458	103.2 s
Mouse Mickey	14710	141.2 s

The results appear as a string of numbers, but they are easy to interpret and now the teacher can ask Billie Jean King why she thinks oily fish is unhealthy. The level of participation in this activity is huge and it is very quick to administer.

Free Text

The development of the free-text function has opened up the use of response technology to teachers who would only rarely use the voting option offered by early systems. The facility for students, however shy or nervous, to be able to contribute via the handsets their words, ideas, variables, feelings, questions, and answers, has the potential to revolutionize participation and motivation.

Once the text function is selected, the students can enter via the keyboard single words, phrases, or even paragraphs of text.

Two examples of the teacher in the healthy eating lesson using the text function are shown below.

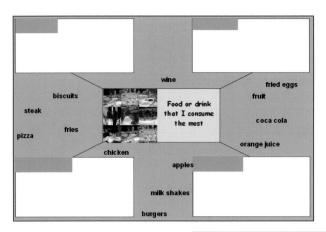

The teacher asks the students to reflect on their eating and drinking habits and to select one item of food or drink that they eat or drink a lot of.

This item should be entered using the text function. The teacher displays the results and immediately seeds them to the screen as in the image on the left. There are 4 boxes on the screen with the heading hidden.

The teacher then reveals the headings of the 4 boxes: "healthy," "not healthy," "ok occasionally," and "depends." She asks students to identify their item and suggest which box the word should be dragged to. The class will debate each suggestion

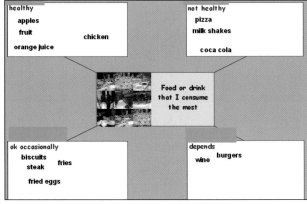

The use of the texting function has guaranteed the participation of all students. The resulting texts can be debated by the class, resulting in deeper understanding of the issues. The finished diagram can be printed out as a poster or handout if written work is to follow.

Self-Paced Learning

What makes ActivExpression revolutionary is its Self-Paced function. Indeed, the phrase Self-Paced does not do it justice. This particular function has so many features that it might have other names: *real-time intervention*, or *differentiated assessment manager*, or even personalized response system. The problem with all of these titles is that not one of them accurately captures the essence of ActivExpression because it offers all of the features that the different titles imply: it does allow students to work at their own pace; it informs teachers and students the moment an error is made, supporting *real-time intervention*; it does allow questions, assessments, and tasks to be *differentiated* so that all students get appropriate degrees of challenge. Put all of these together and you really do have technology that makes the term "*personalized response*" a reality rather than a meaningless sound bite.

This chapter will explore the impact that the Self-Paced function can have on learning and interaction, both in and out of the classroom. Real case studies of its use follow, but this chapter looks in detail at the way it can be used and how the information it provides can be used by teachers, classroom assistants, and students. It will first explore the key functions of the Self-Paced mode and then how it helps to meet challenges familiar to teachers all over the world:

1. Students do not arrive at the classroom at the same time. Teachers wait until all the students are there before starting the lesson, wasting time for those who arrived promptly. (Also see chapter Starting Lessons.)
2. Students in the class have differing levels of skill and confidence, and complete work at different speeds; some are on question 10 before others have passed question 3.
3. More able but lazy students slow down in their work because they know that if they finish too quickly, the teacher will give them additional tasks.
4. Students of all levels of skill record "right" answers by simply copying their friends sat near to them.
5. Plowing through worksheets, students get very little feedback—positive or negative. Because of this, some make the same mistake time and again and will only get guidance after the work is marked or assessed, which may be days later.
6. Feedback to teachers is vital. Who is working well? Who needs help? Who is refusing to participate? Who needs more challenge? In large classes many such issues get missed.
7. When the feedback informs teachers of a problem faced by one or two students, some review that topic by pausing the lesson and others go over it again next lesson. Many students are now wasting time because they already understand and didn't need the reminder.
8. Some teachers do not have the time or energy to create their own questions for a quick assessment in Math.

Basic Functions

Self-Paced

The Self-Paced mode in ActivExpression can be used once teachers decide to plan activities with more than one question or instruction.

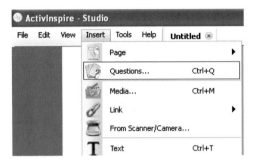

Simply select "Insert" and then "Questions." The Question Manager then appears.

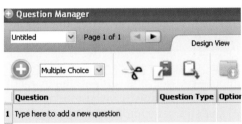

Type in a question, e.g. "How many days in a week?" and then click on the "Question Type" column. Teachers can then choose the type of question:

- Multiple choice
- Yes/No—True/False
- Sort in order
- Likert Scale
- Numeric
- Text

The teacher selects "Text" and enters "7" in the answer column.

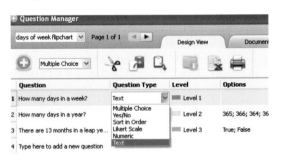

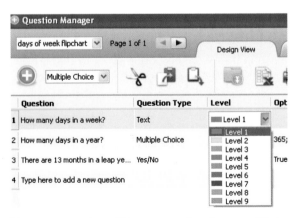

The teacher has chosen a very simple question as Question 1, so Level 1 is now selected from the Level column. This column allows teachers to grade difficulty levels on a 7-point scale.

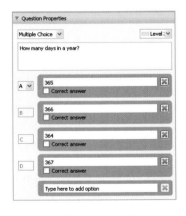

The next question, "How many days in a year?", is multiple choice and Level 2, so the teacher enters the multiple-choice options in the column on the right and ticks the "Correct answer" option.

The teacher only wants four options so clicks on the red Xs to delete options 5 and 6.

28

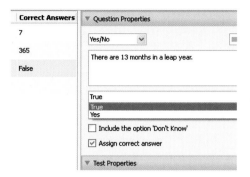

The teacher wants Question 3, "*There are 13 months in a leap year,*" to be a "True/False" so selects "Yes/No" and then clicks on "Yes" in the right column to reveal the "True/False" option.

Teachers may decide to have multiple questions at each level of difficulty. In the example below, the teacher has five questions at each of Level 1, Level 2, and Level 3.

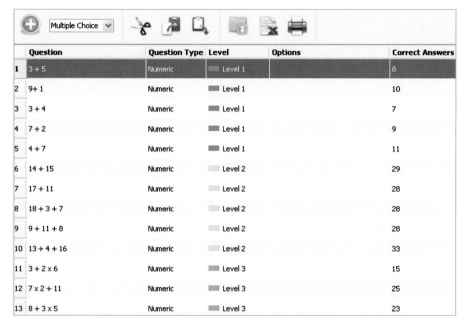

	Question	Question Type	Level	Options	Correct Answers
1	3 + 5	Numeric	Level 1		8
2	9 + 1	Numeric	Level 1		10
3	3 + 4	Numeric	Level 1		7
4	7 + 2	Numeric	Level 1		9
5	4 + 7	Numeric	Level 1		11
6	14 + 15	Numeric	Level 2		29
7	17 + 11	Numeric	Level 2		28
8	18 + 3 + 7	Numeric	Level 2		28
9	9 + 11 + 8	Numeric	Level 2		28
10	13 + 4 + 16	Numeric	Level 2		33
11	$3 + 2 \times 6$	Numeric	Level 3		15
12	$7 \times 2 + 11$	Numeric	Level 3		25
13	$8 + 3 \times 5$	Numeric	Level 3		23

It may be desirable, however, for students who answer correctly to move up a level without having to do all of the questions within that level.

Teachers can also choose to have the questions *within* a level sent to the handsets in a random order, so that one student, for example, might get Level 1 questions in this order: 5-2-3-1-4. Another might get the same questions in this order: 1-3-2-5-4. The randomize option prevents one student from simply copying the text entries of a friend.

The "Control through levels" and "Randomize" options can be found by selecting the "Test Properties" tab in the right-hand column. In this example, the teacher has set the movement between levels at four correct answers and the questions are not randomized.

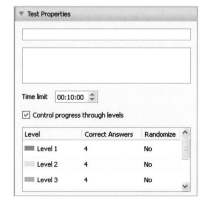

Basic Functions

Finally, once the questions are all prepared, teachers now have the option of adding a response to students as they answer them. Teachers, if they choose, can set up a response for each question that is correct and one for each one that is incorrect. The wording of the response can be a simple: "correct" or "incorrect." However, teachers can also choose to individualize the response with positive phrases such as "brilliant," "you're a wiz," "well done," or "congratulations" when the answer is correct. If incorrect, then teachers can insert "sorry, try another," "think again," or, as one teacher in the case study section of the book chose, "urghh!" Many current users of ActivExpresion only use the "incorrect" option, telling students *"If you don't get a message then assume you are right."*

The response option is found in the right-hand column under *"Test Feedback Properties."* If none of the boxes are selected, then no response is sent to the handset.

Finally, in that same menu is the option for teachers to "Send Summary" to each handset at the end of an assessment, telling students where they came in the overall test, e.g. *"Your current position is 1 of 32, answering 19 questions correctly in 57 seconds."*

3 + 5	
Correct answer	8
Tolerance +/-	0
☑ Assign correct answer	

▶ Test Properties

▼ Test Feedback Properties

Send message to learner when

☐ Answer correct	Correct
☑ Answer incorrect	Sorry, not correct
☐ Send summary	

▶ Flipchart Page Properties

Finally, when the questions are ready and the option choices selected, the Self-Paced activity can begin.

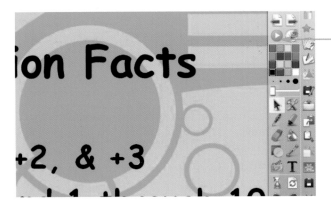

ion Facts

+2, & +3

The green arrow shows that the Self-Paced activity is ready to start. Click on it and the questions go directly to the handset screen of each individual student.

1

How many vertices are there on a square based pyramid?

◀Answer

As soon as individual students are ready to answer, they press "answer," enter their answer or response, and "send." If it is correct and the teacher has not programmed a response, then another question is sent to the screen immediately. It does not wait for other students to respond. That is why the term Self-Paced is used. Within a minute, some students are on question 5 while others are still on questions 1 or 2.

Meeting Challenges

Once users have mastered the basic functions of the Self-Paced mode, they will be ready to see at first hand how the ActivExpression technology can meet some of the challenges outlined in the introduction to this chapter.

Challenge 1

Students do not arrive at the classroom at the same time. Teachers wait until all the students are there before starting the lesson, wasting time for those who arrive promptly. (More examples of this can be found in the chapter Starting Lessons.)

The Self-Paced mode is an ideal way of starting lessons so that learning begins on entry to the classroom. For this to be effective, the ActivExpression handsets need to be available on entry to the classroom, and already registered with the hub. The names of the students are not important at this stage—they can be added later. The schools from the United Church Schools Trust in the UK use storage cabinets like the one here to make the handsets easily accessible on entry.

Students pick up a handset on arrival, sit down, switch on the power, and immediately start the Self-Paced activity. They are instantly quiet and settled, and the teacher is able to monitor the responses of all students live as they work. The example below illustrates this use of Self-Paced.

Aims of the starter

In the previous lesson, the class had been introduced to electrical circuits and had done some short, practical experiments on setting up serial and parallel circuits. The teacher was planning to develop this topic further and the starting activity is to show what they can remember from the previous lesson.

The questions

There are five Self-Paced questions in the starter. The questions are set out below.

This starter, linked with ongoing work, engaged learners with a task that required them to show what they had learned about electrical circuits.

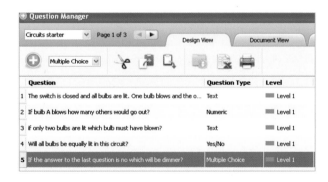

Once the activity is over, the teacher brings up the class list and PINs (or uses the rename function), and the handsets are registered with names. The data from this exercise will influence how much revision is needed with individuals or the class before moving on to further work on circuits.

Grateful thanks to the United Church Schools Trust in the UK for permission to adapt some flipchart pages from their forthcoming training materials "ActivExpression for Learning."

Meeting Challenges

Challenge 2

Students in the class have differing levels of skill and confidence, and complete work at different speeds; some are on question 10 before others have passed question 3.

The differentiation of teaching techniques and learning activities is a major challenge for all teachers, even those who teach classes grouped by ability. No group of students is totally homogeneous and the challenge to meet the needs of individuals is daunting to many, even experienced practitioners. Self-Paced learning addresses some of those needs.

In the Math Self-Paced activity below, the teacher has recognized that there are learners in the class who find percentages very difficult and others who are brilliant at Math and need challenges. The questions below are a selection of the prepared Self-Paced set. In the original, there were 55 questions with at least six questions at each level, but in order to demonstrate the range, only two at each level are shown.

The diagram (right) demonstrates a key issue: How quickly or slowly students work. It is an extract from the live feedback that Self-Paced provides and is a snapshot of a test 3 minutes after the start. Some are on Q5, others on Q14!

	Question	Question Type	Level
4	10% of 50	Numeric	Level 2
5	100% of 425	Numeric	Level 2
6	45% of 800?	Numeric	Level 3
7	25% of 600?	Numeric	Level 3
8	150% as a fraction?	Text	Level 4
9	125% as a fraction	Text	Level 4
10	Ed's salary is $24,000. It increases by 4%. What is it now in £s?	Numeric	Level 5
11	Ed's salary is $24,000. It increases by 6%. What is it now in £s?	Numeric	Level 5
12	Dan buys a $40 game and gets 40% discount. What does he pay i...	Numeric	Level 6
13	Jim invests $4500 at compound interest of 5% pa. After n comple...	Numeric	Level 7
14	I invest $2500 at 1%pa roughly (+/-) how much ($s) will I have in...	Numeric	Level 7
15	John bought a ring abroad for Tracy it was $420 plus tax @ 17.5...	Numeric	Level 8

The students who find Math easy will be onto higher level questions very quickly, and for some it will be competitive as they "race" other students to complete the 55 questions in the original test. Other students will progress at "their own pace," regardless and oblivious to the progress of others. The remarkable feature of such lessons is the intense concentration of the students, with eyes only for their own handset screens. Not only that, they are working on tasks that are appropriate and differentiated.

Meeting Challenges

Challenge 3
More able but lazy students slow down in their work because they know that if they finish too quickly, the teacher will give them additional tasks.

Many teachers will have come across the situation when, a quarter of the way through the lesson, an able student walks up and says "I've finished!" The teacher says "*well done*," lets out a sigh of frustration and says to the student "*do 20 more*." The student then walks away muttering "*I'll slow down next time*." It is amazing how 20 questions on a worksheet can have this negative impact upon motivation, and yet in Self-Paced there is a totally different reaction. The example below serves as an illustration.

As the author of this book, I undertook some research in the USA and the UK, and was privileged to watch the lesson described here. The 13-year-olds in this Math lesson were studying the topic "Graphing quadratic functions" and were required to work in pairs. A range of 20 graphs were displayed labeled A–T and a set of Self-Paced questions had been prepared from Level 1 to Level 9. The students had to match the question to the graph. For example, the answer to Q4 is P.

	Question	Question Type	Level
3	$x^2 - 3$	Text	Level 1
4	$x^2 - 7x + 10$	Text	Level 2
5	$-x^2 - 2x + 1$	Text	Level 2
6	$-x^2 - 2x - 1$	Text	Level 3
7	$x^2 - 3x - 5$	Text	Level 3
8	$-3x^2 - x + 2$	Text	Level 4
9	$-x^2 + 3x - 2$	Text	Level 4
10	$1/3 x^2 - 4$	Text	Level 5
11	$3x^2 + 4$	Text	Level 5
12	$-3x^2 + 4$	Text	Level 6
13	$-1/3 x^2 - 3$	Text	Level 6
14	$1/4 x^2 - 3$	Text	Level 7
15	$2x^2 + x - 3$	Text	Level 7
16	$x^2 - 2x - 3$	Text	Level 8

The use of ActivExpression here in its Self-Paced mode had a huge impact upon the motivation of the students and the pace of the work.

I have to confess that in 38 years of being a teacher and a Principal, I have never seen a group of students work with such intensity, concentration, and pace over such a lengthy period; 45 minutes with not a wasted second.

The live feedback (see later section) the teacher was getting on her screen told her which pair was on which question, and she constantly relayed this message to her class. "*Pair 5 is now in the lead*," she would say and students would express dismay and redouble their efforts.

The live feedback enabled the teacher to identify problems quickly and she regularly intervened with a few prompts and hints. Every time students sent in a correct answer, the message on the handset screen congratulated them and another question was instantly sent.

My thanks to Lakesha Goff from the Ron Clark Academy in Atlanta for allowing me to observe this stunning lesson.

Meeting Challenges

Challenge 4
Many students, of all levels of skill, record "right" answers by simply copying their friends sat near to them.

All kinds of students copy work: lazy, anxious, demotivated, and weak learners will resort to this practice on occasion and this makes it very difficult for teachers to assess progress because some of them will have "right" answers but no understanding. One of the features of the Self-Paced mode tackles this problem in an ingenious way. It's the "*randomize*" function.

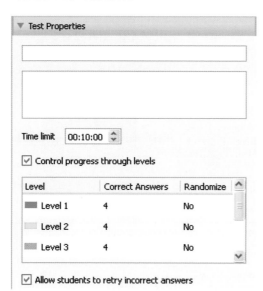

When the teacher plans the Self-Paced question set, there is a "*Test Properties*" option in the right-hand panel.

Select this and you will see the "Control progress through levels" box, which should be ticked.

This then allows teachers to decide how many correct answers students need to get before advancing to the next level.

Next to it is the "*Randomize*" option. Select "Yes" and the software will send questions from within a level in a random order.

If the randomize option is selected then the questions below from each level will appear on students' handsets in a random order, so that two students sitting alongside each other are almost certainly seeing different questions. This makes copying very difficult.

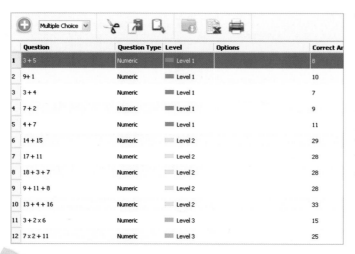

This will also have a major impact upon learning. Students who do not understand will make errors or take a long time over each question. Both of these situations will be obvious to the teacher watching the live feedback on the computer screen, and intervention can take place.

Meeting Challenges

Challenge 5

Plowing through worksheets, students get very little feedback, positive or negative. Because of this, some make the same mistake time and again and will only get guidance after the work is marked or assessed, which may be days later. Good feedback to teachers will enable intervention when it is needed.

Feedback in any form of life is important for a number of reasons. Positive feedback helps to maintain motivation and provides reassurance that you are proceeding on the right lines. Feedback which identifies areas of concern or errors helps individuals to modify their practice or seek help to do so. The absence of feedback in learning situations, therefore, can impact upon everyone including the teacher, who may be unaware that the teaching has not been effective and that a change of plan is needed. ActivExpression is revolutionary because it provides *live* and *instant* feedback to learners, support assistants, and teachers.

Example1: Progress bar graph

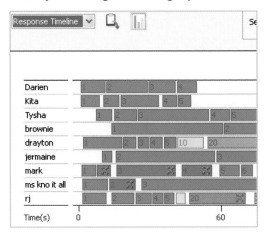

Bar graph

Feedback in ActivExpression is provided in a number of ways.

As each student responds, a *bar graph* next to their name moves. The longer the bar on each question, the longer they took to answer. What does this progress chart tell us?

- brownie took a long time over Q1– nearly 60 seconds.
- The change of color indicates a level change. Drayton has gone up two levels.

Intervention

The progress bar graph is only the start of the feedback. The bar graph tells us mark is struggling because his chart has 3 Xs on Q1, Q2, and Q3.

If the teacher hovers the cursor over any of these, it shows what mark answered. In Q3 he was confusing percentages with subtraction and the teacher intervened immediately. Q5, Q6, and Q7 are now all right!

The teacher also intervened with ms kno it all on Q2, and Q3 is now correct.

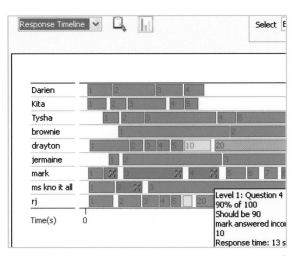

Meeting Challenges

Challenge 6

Feedback to teachers is vital. Who is working well? Who needs help? Who is refusing to participate? Who needs more challenge? In large classes, many such issued get missed.

Sometimes in lessons, one or more students for a variety of reasons decide they do not want to try or to participate. When Self-Paced mode is in use, this is easy to spot.

The feedback in this image shows how one student has a string of crosses without any delay between them. It shows how any answer is being sent without thought. The teacher will be able to intervene and see what the problem is.

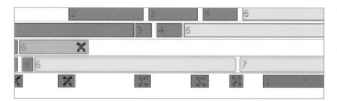

The white line here tells the teacher that one student has just switched off the handset or failed to press "clear" after the message! A quick chat is in order.

The black cross here tells the teacher that the student has retried Q6 and got it wrong twice. Intervention is needed.

The Self-Paced mode also provides a detailed analysis of students' performance individually: levels tackled, number of questions right or wrong, and time taken.

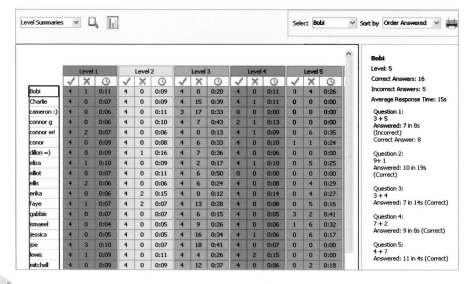

	Level 1			Level 2			Level 3			Level 4			Level 5		
	✓	✗	🕐	✓	✗	🕐	✓	✗	🕐	✓	✗	🕐	✓	✗	🕐
Bobi	4	1	0:11	4	0	0:09	4	0	0:20	4	0	0:11	0	4	0:26
Charlie	4	0	0:07	4	0	0:09	4	15	0:39	4	1	0:11	0	0	0:00
cameron :)	4	0	0:06	4	0	0:11	3	17	0:33	0	0	0:00	0	0	0:00
connor g	4	0	0:06	4	0	0:10	4	7	0:43	2	1	0:13	0	0	0:00
connor w!	4	2	0:07	4	0	0:06	4	0	0:13	4	1	0:09	0	6	0:35
conor	4	0	0:09	4	0	0:08	4	6	0:33	4	0	0:10	1	1	0:24
dillon =)	4	0	0:09	4	1	0:16	4	7	0:36	4	0	0:06	0	0	0:00
eliza	4	1	0:10	4	0	0:09	4	2	0:17	4	1	0:10	0	5	0:25
elliot	4	0	0:07	4	0	0:11	4	6	0:50	0	0	0:00	0	0	0:00
ellis	4	2	0:06	4	0	0:06	4	6	0:24	4	0	0:08	0	4	0:29
erika	4	0	0:06	4	2	0:15	4	0	0:12	4	0	0:14	0	4	0:27
faye	4	1	0:07	4	2	0:07	4	13	0:28	4	0	0:08	0	5	0:16
gabbie	4	0	0:07	4	0	0:07	4	6	0:15	4	0	0:05	3	2	0:41
ismaeel	4	0	0:04	4	0	0:05	4	9	0:26	4	0	0:06	1	6	0:32
jessica	4	0	0:05	4	0	0:05	4	16	0:34	4	1	0:06	0	6	0:17
joe	4	3	0:10	4	0	0:07	4	18	0:41	4	0	0:07	0	0	0:00
lewis	4	1	0:09	4	0	0:11	4	4	0:26	4	2	0:15	0	0	0:00
mitchell	4	0	0:09	4	0	0:09	4	12	0:37	4	0	0:06	0	2	0:18

Level Summaries · Select Bobi · Sort by Order Answered

Bobi
Level: 5
Correct Answers: 16
Incorrect Answers: 5
Average Response Time: 15s

Question 1:
3 + 5
Answered: 7 in 8s
(Incorrect)
Correct Answer: 8

Question 2:
9 + 1
Answered: 10 in 19s
(Correct)

Question 3:
3 + 4
Answered: 7 in 14s (Correct)

Question 4:
7 + 2
Answered: 9 in 8s (Correct)

Question 5:
4 + 7
Answered: 11 in 4s (Correct)

Meeting Challenges

Challenge 7

When the feedback informs teachers of a problem faced by one or two students, some review that topic by pausing the lesson and others go over it again next lesson. Many students are now wasting time because they already understand and didn't need the reminder.

Using feedback in lesson planning

Good teachers get feedback in all kinds of ways and then use that feedback to act in some way that benefits learners:

- Modifying the lesson to revisit a topic that has obviously caused learners problems.
- Inviting a small group with similar problems to join the teacher for a short tutorial.
- Providing another group of students, who are finding the tasks easy, with a set of more challenging questions.
- Making changes to the following lesson plan in order to meet the needs that the feedback has identified.

Traditional marking of work, however, makes most of this very difficult. If, for example, teachers wanted to know which questions caused the class most problems, it would take hours to trawl through piles of work books, test sheets, or folders, time that simply isn't there in the hectic world of teaching. Electronic analysis, however, transforms this search.

The feedback already described provides rich data on the progress of students, and it can also analyze the questions and how students coped with them.

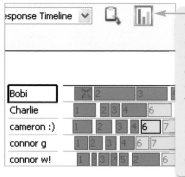

Select a question, e.g. Q6 (highlighted on flipchart), and click on the bar graph icon at the top; this will provide an instant analysis of how many students were correct.

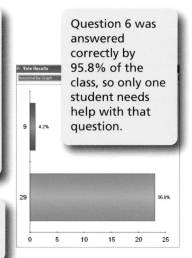

Question 6 was answered correctly by 95.8% of the class, so only one student needs help with that question.

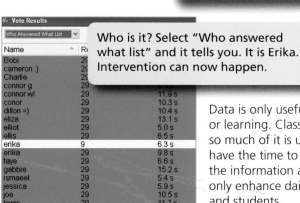

Who is it? Select "Who answered what list" and it tells you. It is Erika. Intervention can now happen.

Data is only useful if it is used to enhance teaching or learning. Classrooms are rich in information, but so much of it is unused because teachers do not have the time to access it. ActivExpression makes the information available instantly and easily. It can only enhance daily classroom life for both teachers and students.

The Response Revolution

Meeting Challenges

Challenge 8
Some teachers do not have the time or energy to create their own questions for a quick assessment in Math.

Many teachers like to create their own assessments to meet the various needs of their students, and that is to be applauded. In Math, however, particularly for areas of basic numeracy skills in adding, subtracting, dividing, and multiplying, creating such tests or practice questions can be very time-consuming. The Self-Paced mode in ActivExpression has an answer for this—the *Question Generator*.

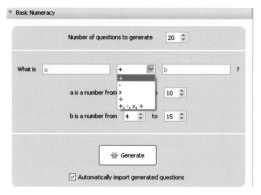

Select "Insert" on the flipchart and then "Questions," and the screen on the left appears. The drop-down screen provides the option of +, -, x, ÷, or a combination of all of them.

Select the number range for "a" and "b" and the number of questions for the test, and click on "Generate."

The questions will appear on the right screen as in the example below.

All of these questions are at Level 1, and for rapid practice of tables or adding, for example, this is fine. If teachers want to have a range of challenges, however, the Question Generator allows teachers to generate and select a range of levels.

	Question	Question Type	Level	Options	Corr
1	4 + 11	Numeric	Level 1		15
2	7 + 7	Numeric	Level 1		14
3	4 + 10	Numeric	Level 1		14
4	3 + 13	Numeric	Level 1		16
5	7 + 13	Numeric	Level 1		20
6	5 + 8	Numeric	Level 1		13
7	5 + 7	Numeric	Level 1		12
8	5 + 6	Numeric	Level 1		11
9	6 + 14	Numeric	Level 1		20
10	9 + 6	Numeric	Level 1		15

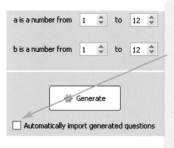

To select questions, open the Question Generator and untick "Automatically import generated questions." Select the number of questions, the type of calculation, and the number ranges for "a" and "b." Select "Generate."

Once the questions appear, use the "control" key to select the questions you want and then select the orange icon "Import" and "Done." Repeat the process with harder calculations and you will have a customized set.

To apply the levels to each group of questions, select "Edit" and then "Questions on current page," and use the "control" key to highlight all the Level 1 questions. Select Level 1 in the "Question Properties" on the right-hand side and then repeat for other sets at different levels.

Starting Lessons

"Start as you mean to go on" is a phrase I often use when I am working with trainee teachers, but the principles behind these words should apply to all educators. First impressions are critical in many walks of life and in many contexts: the smile on arrival at Reception, the quick response from customer service to a telephone query, the email to thank you after you have helped someone—all offer a subliminal message that makes you feel positive towards the organization or person concerned.

Effective teachers establish and constantly reinforce these subliminal messages: in the way they address colleagues, students, and parents; in the way they manage and respond to interaction in their classrooms; and in the way in which feedback to student learning provides both encouragement and challenge.

One of the most effective ways in which teachers establish this ethos is at the beginning of lessons. Let me start with a few statistics:

1. In many High Schools, lessons last approximately one hour and there are six lessons a day. This means that with break and lunch periods accounted for, there will be a minimum of three periods of transition between lessons each day. Some schools organize shorter lessons of approximately 35 or 40 minutes, and in these schools there may be up to six transitions a day excluding formal breaks.

2. In many schools the time gap between the first student arriving in the classroom and the last one arriving is between five and ten minutes, which for the sake of argument I will average out at seven and a half minutes.

3. If the teacher starts the learning activity when the last student has arrived, then the following represents the "wait" or "non-learning" time:

   3 periods of transition x 7.5 minutes = 22.5 minutes each day

   5 days a week x 22.5 minutes = 1 hour 52.5 minutes a week

   38 weeks a year x 1 hour 52.5 minutes = 71.25 hours

   5 years (e.g. ages 11–16) 5 x 71.25 hours = 12 weeks of wasted time

If the waiting time is 10 minutes per lesson then the final figure is 15 weeks! The figure for lost time in schools that operate 35-minute lessons is too horrendous to calculate. It is not only the waste of learning time, however, that is at issue. An unproductive, 10-minute waiting time can easily deteriorate into an unsettling period of low-level disruption, rising noise levels, and increased classroom tension—hardly conducive to the learning that is to follow. That is why some schools introduce draconian "rules" such as those that require students on arrival to stand silently behind their desks until the teacher is ready to start.

INTRODUCTION

Expecting newly arrived students to stand behind their desks in silence until the last one arrives may afford a degree of "control" but has little else to commend it. Behind this form of control is a desire on the part of the teacher or the school to create a well-ordered and calm atmosphere which will help to create the conditions for effective learning and teaching. There are much better ways to achieve this laudable goal.

Many schools in the UK and elsewhere have introduced the concept of "lesson starters." These are designed to create a well-ordered and calm atmosphere; they are widely used in some schools and can become a useful strategy in the right situation. My concern with "starters" is that in many schools they have become a set-in-concrete school rule—all teachers must plan lessons with a "starter."

This is complete nonsense for some, e.g. teachers of Art and Design. In most Art lessons students know what they are doing, and arrive wanting to get out their portfolio of work and simply carry on. The starter in this situation is a distraction and totally unnecessary, and the same will apply to any lesson where students are in the middle of an ongoing piece of work and don't need to be diverted from their prime purpose.

Another issue that I have with starters is that often the activity has no connection to the previous learning of that class or to the learning for the lesson which is about to start. The best lessons, I am sure, are seamless; from the moment learners walk through the door they are engaged in activities that are purposeful and coherent.

This section of the book includes a range of ways in which teachers can "start as they mean to go on" by adopting short, focused activities that motivate learners and create the atmosphere and conditions for later learning. The examples address not only the focus of the learning but the ways in which students' minds are occupied as soon as they arrive, and the use of ActivExpression, particularly its Self-Paced function, provides opportunities in this respect that are unrivalled in the world of educational technology.

Aims of the starter

In the previous lesson the class had been introduced to the history of the Civil Rights movement in the USA and had read and talked about the story of Rosa Parks and the bus boycott in Alabama. The teacher was planning to develop this topic further and the starting activity is used to show what they can remember from the previous lesson.

Target teaching group

Ages 13–16

Context

The handsets are collected as students walk through the door. The interactive whiteboard screen has been frozen with the information below.

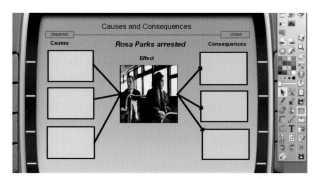

The handsets have been registered with the hub and the Self-Paced activity has been activated by the teacher. As soon as each learner sits down and switches on ActivExpression, the questions begin. At this stage no names have been registered so responses are anonymous. The learners start answering the questions.

The questions

There are 4 Self-Paced questions in the starter. The questions are set out below.

The responses will be seeded to the screen as soon as the last student has arrived and settled, or when the teacher judges the time is right. They will be dragged into the boxes by the teacher and students will be invited to explain their entries. The topic will then be developed further.

This starter linked with ongoing work, engaging learners with a task that required them to show both their understanding and their emotions. The discussion that is generated by the seeding of the words and feelings will be a good introduction to the new lesson but will also highlight any misconceptions held by students from the earlier lesson.

Grateful thanks to the United Church Schools Trust in the UK for permission to adapt some flipchart pages from their forthcoming training materials "ActivExpression for Learning."

Healthy Eating

Aims of the starter

The class was introduced to the theme of "Living Healthily" in the previous lesson and in this lesson the teacher plans to introduce the issues of nutrition. The starter is a means of getting them to practice the skills of reading tables of data prior to the main lesson, when the meanings of the words and their links to healthy living will be explored.

Target teaching group

Ages 9–11

Context

The handsets are collected as students walk through the door. The interactive whiteboard screen has been frozen with the table of information below.

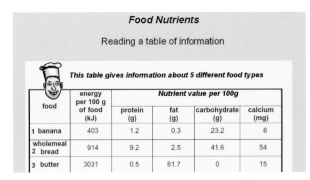

Food Nutrients

Reading a table of information

This table gives information about 5 different food types

food	energy per 100 g of food (kJ)	Nutrient value per 100g			
		protein (g)	fat (g)	carbohydrate (g)	calcium (mg)
1 banana	403	1.2	0.3	23.2	6
2 wholemeal bread	914	9.2	2.5	41.6	54
3 butter	3031	0.5	81.7	0	15

The handsets have been registered with the hub and the Self-Paced activity has been activated by the teacher. As soon as each learner sits down and switches on ActivExpression, the questions begin. At this stage no names have been registered so responses are anonymous. The learners start answering the questions.

The questions

There are 5 Self-Paced questions in the set. The questions are set out on the right.

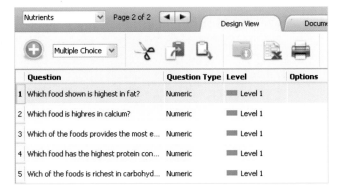

| | Nutrients | Page 2 of 2 | | | Design View | | Docume |

	Question	Question Type	Level	Options
1	Which food shown is highest in fat?	Numeric	Level 1	
2	Which food is highres in calcium?	Numeric	Level 1	
3	Which of the foods provides the most e...	Numeric	Level 1	
4	Which food has the highest protein con...	Numeric	Level 1	
5	Wich of the foods is richest in carbohyd...	Numeric	Level 1	

The responses will be brought up on the screen as soon as the last student has arrived and settled, or when the teacher judges the time is right. They will be used by the teacher to show how to read the table and to explore what the learners already know about the words in the table.

This starter linked with ongoing work, engaging learners with a task that required them to interpret information from a table of data and then select the appropriate answer. Once the activity is over, the teacher brings up the class list and PINs, and the handsets are registered with names.

Grateful thanks to the United Church Schools Trust in the UK for permission to adapt some flipchart pages from their forthcoming training materials "ActivExpression for Learning."

Making Analogies

Aims of the starter

Using analogies is an established technique for honing and developing thinking skills. Ten analogies are presented and pupils have to select, from a choice of four, the correct word to complete the analogy. It is being used as a mental warm-up activity that leads into the development of analogies to support thinking, and the creation of analogies to support learning across a particular topic or theme.

Target teaching group

Ages 7–11

Context

The handsets are collected as students walk through the door. The interactive whiteboard screen has been frozen with the information below.

The handsets have been registered with the hub and the Self-Paced activity has been activated by the teacher. As soon as each learner sits down and switches on ActivExpression, the questions begin. At this stage no names have been registered so responses are anonymous. The learners start making their selections.

The questions

There are 10 Self-Paced questions in the set. The questions are set out on the right.

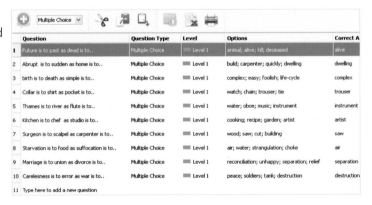

	Question	Question Type	Level	Options	Correct A
1	Future is to past as dead is to..	Multiple Choice	Level 1	animal; alive; kill; deceased	alive
2	Abrupt is to sudden as home is to..	Multiple Choice	Level 1	build; carpenter; quickly; dwelling	dwelling
3	birth is to death as simple is to..	Multiple Choice	Level 1	complex; easy; foolish; life-cycle	complex
4	Collar is to shirt as pocket is to..	Multiple Choice	Level 1	watch; chain; trouser; tie	trouser
5	Thames is to river as flute is to..	Multiple Choice	Level 1	water; oboe; music; instrument	instrument
6	Kitchen is to chef as studio is to..	Multiple Choice	Level 1	cooking; recipe; garden; artist	artist
7	Surgeon is to scalpel as carpenter is to..	Multiple Choice	Level 1	wood; saw; cut; building	saw
8	Starvation is to food as suffocation is to..	Multiple Choice	Level 1	air; water; strangulation; choke	air
9	Marriage is to union as divorce is to..	Multiple Choice	Level 1	reconciliation; unhappy; separation; relief	separation
10	Carelessness is to error as war is to..	Multiple Choice	Level 1	peace; soldiers; tank; destruction	destruction
11	Type here to add a new question				

The responses will be brought up on the screen as soon as the last student has arrived and settled, or when the teacher judges the time is right. They will be used by the teacher to develop discussion over the choices made and as an introduction to further work on this topic. This starter linked with ongoing work, engaging learners with a task that required them to read carefully, to think, and then to select the appropriate answer. Once the activity is over, the teacher brings up the class list and PINs and the handsets are registered with names.

Grateful thanks to the United Church Schools Trust in the UK for permission to adapt some flipchart pages from their forthcoming training materials "ActivExpression for Learning."

Soccer statistics

Aims of the starter

There are two key aims of this starting activity: (1) To give students practice in distinguishing between the terms mean, mode, and median in soccer statistics (motivating!), and (2) to encourage them to arrive on time. A secondary activity after the starter awards merit points to the students who do best on the test, and getting there first gives them an advantage!

Target teaching group

Ages 13–14. The class has already had a lesson on the terms mean, mode, and median.

Context

The handsets are collected as students walk through the door. The interactive whiteboard screen has been frozen with the table of soccer statistics below.

Player		Goals scored	Assists
A.	Rooney	10	11
B.	Torres	10	6
C.	Van Persie	16	7
D.	Drogba	12	15

Premier soccer league statistics for season 2010/11

The handsets have been registered with the hub and the Self-Paced activity has been activated by the teacher. As soon as each learner sits down and switches on ActivExpression, the questions begin. At this stage no names have been registered so responses are anonymous. The learners start answering the questions.

The questions

There are 12 Self-Paced questions in the starter, Levels 1 to 4, set out below.

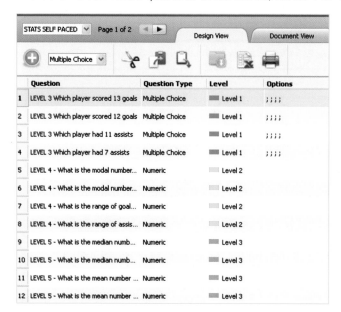

	Question	Question Type	Level	Options
1	LEVEL 3 Which player scored 13 goals	Multiple Choice	Level 1	;;;;
2	LEVEL 3 Which player scored 12 goals	Multiple Choice	Level 1	;;;;
3	LEVEL 3 Which player had 11 assists	Multiple Choice	Level 1	;;;;
4	LEVEL 3 Which player had 7 assists	Multiple Choice	Level 1	;;;;
5	LEVEL 4 - What is the modal number...	Numeric	Level 2	
6	LEVEL 4 - What is the modal number...	Numeric	Level 2	
7	LEVEL 4 - What is the range of goal...	Numeric	Level 2	
8	LEVEL 4 - What is the range of assis...	Numeric	Level 2	
9	LEVEL 5 - What is the median numb...	Numeric	Level 3	
10	LEVEL 5 - What is the median numb...	Numeric	Level 3	
11	LEVEL 5 - What is the mean number ...	Numeric	Level 3	
12	LEVEL 5 - What is the mean number ...	Numeric	Level 3	

The responses will be brought up on the screen as soon as the last student has arrived and settled, or when the teacher judges the time is right.

The Self-Paced question set has been set to send a summary to each handset and the teacher asks who came "top" in the test, who came "second," etc. They are allowed to have first guesses at the secondary activity to win the merits.

Soccer statistics

This starter activity is motivating, fast-paced, and linked to the learning that has gone previously and with the learning that will follow. But it also has the benefit of encouraging prompt arrival at the lesson, because the students start as soon as they sit down and do not have to wait for the latecomers. There is an additional incentive for the students. Once the activity is stopped by the teacher, the summary on the handset informs each student how they fared in the class—1st, 2nd, 3rd, etc.

The teacher turns to the next page on the flipchart and there are 20 boxes. In 3 of the boxes there are hidden some merit awards—3 merits, 2 merits, and 1 merit.

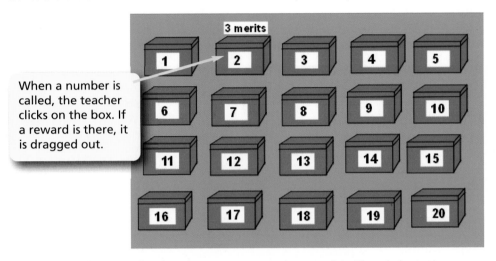

When a number is called, the teacher clicks on the box. If a reward is there, it is dragged out.

The student who came first has three guesses at a box number. The student who came second has two guesses and the remainder of the class has one guess until all 3 merit awards are found. The chances are that more than half the class will have a guess, rewarding them (a) for their Math skills, and (b) for arriving at the lesson promptly.

The idea of providing incentives does not have to involve rewards. The same teacher has another activity which asks students to text in two letters to spot similar triangles frozen on the screen. A face is hidden behind. Who is it today?

Once the teacher has received sufficient responses, individuals are asked to drag the similar triangles to the dustbin. After doing so, they try to guess who the face is behind the triangles. After selecting pairs BF, DG, HP, the next student chose KN and was able to see it was John Kennedy! The puzzle element to this makes the activity highly motivating.

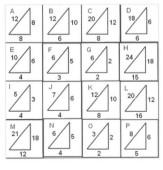

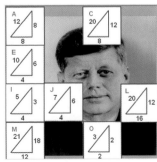

Thanks to Ben Matthews, Walkden High School, Manchester, UK, for these two examples.

Circuits

Aims of the starter

In the previous lesson, the class had been introduced to electrical circuits and had done some short, practical experiments on setting up serial and parallel circuits. The teacher was planning to develop this topic further and the starting activity is to show what they can remember from the previous lesson.

Target teaching group

Ages 11–12

Context

The handsets are collected as students walk through the door. The interactive whiteboard screen has been frozen with the information below.

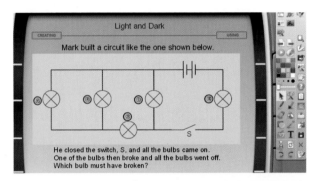

The handsets have been registered with the hub and the Self-Paced activity has been activated by the teacher. As soon as each learner sits down and switches on ActivExpression, the questions begin. At this stage no names have been registered so responses are anonymous. The learners start answering the questions.

The questions

There are 5 Self-Paced questions in the starter. The questions are set out on the right.

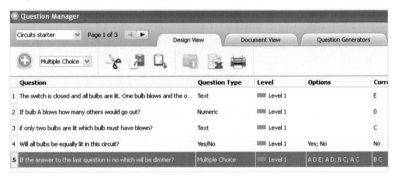

Question	Question Type	Level	Options	Corre
1 The switch is closed and all bulbs are lit. One bulb blows and the o...	Text	Level 1		E
2 If bulb A blows how many others would go out?	Numeric	Level 1		0
3 If only two bulbs are lit which bulb must have blown?	Text	Level 1		C
4 Will all bulbs be equally lit in this circuit?	Yes/No	Level 1	Yes; No	No
5 If the answer to the last question is no which will be dimmer?	Multiple Choice	Level 1	A D E; A D; B C; A C	B C

The responses will be brought up on the screen as soon as the last student has arrived and settled, or when the teacher judges the time is right. They will be used by the teacher to determine how many students have understood the principles of circuits from the previous lesson.

This starter linked with ongoing work, engaging learners with a task that required them to show what they had learned about electrical circuits. Once the activity is over the teacher brings up the class list and PINs and the handsets are registered with names. The data from this exercise will influence how much revision is needed with individuals or the whole class before moving onto further work on circuits.

Grateful thanks to the United Church Schools Trust in the UK for permission to adapt some flipchart pages from their forthcoming training materials "ActivExpression for Learning."

Aims of the starter
In the previous lesson, the teacher introduced the class to the language of basic directions in French, and this activity at the start of the next lesson is for students to practice their skills and for the teacher to decide if they are ready to progress to using prepositions.

Target teaching group
This is targeted at 10–12-years-olds.

Context
In the previous lesson, students learned places in the town, cardinal numbers, 1st, 2nd, and 3rd, and streets on the right and left. They have practiced them in oral work.

How does the lesson work?
The teacher has prepared a flipchart with a street and buildings including shops, a church, a hospital, a railway station, a café, a post office, and a bank. Self-Paced questions in French have been prepared from Level 1 to Level 3. The flipchart is frozen on the screen and the Self-Paced mode begins.

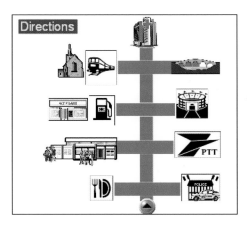

This idea of using an existing image and creating Self-Paced questions to go with it means that teachers of a foreign language might do this for family trees, shopping, transport, sports, and so on. Course books usually have excellent images and some of the questions can also be converted into Self-Paced.

Examples of the type of Self-Paced questions are below.

The assessment, which involves all the students, will inform the teacher what has been mastered before introducing prepositions for giving and receiving directions.

	en ville Page 2 of 3 ◄ ► Design View Document View Question Generators		
	Question	Question Type	Level
1	Où est la poste, s'il vous plaît? Prenez la…	Multiple Choice	Level 1
2	Où est le café, s'il vous plaît? Prenez la..	Multiple Choice	Level 1
3	Où est la gare, s'il vous plaît? Prenez la..	Multiple Choice	Level 2
4	Où est l'église, s'il vous plaît?	Multiple Choice	Level 2
5	Où est l'école, s'il vous plaît? Prenez la ….	Text	Level 3
6	Où est le pont, s'il vous plaît? Prenez la …	Text	Level 3
7	Où est l'hôpital, s'il vous plaît?	Text	Level 3
8	Où est le commisariat, s'il vous plaît? Prenez la ..	Text	Level 3

Thanks to Gail Lambert for this contribution.

Give us a clue French

Aims of the starter

This is the final lesson of this topic on "Directions" and the teacher wants to assess the progress with some writing in the second half of the lesson. She starts the lesson, however, with an engaging activity.

Target teaching group

This idea uses the "Give us a clue" concept in a foreign language lesson. It can be any language so the text in this description will be in English. ·

Context

This activity would be a good follow-up to the two En Ville lessons, one earlier in this section on Starting Lessons, and one in the Ending Lessons section. The students have been taught and practiced the language of directions, 1st, 2nd, 3rd, and *turn right*, *turn left*, *straight ahead*, etc. They have also learned about the use of prepositions such as opposite, next to, etc.

How does the lesson work?

The students, in pairs, are asked to select a place on the map displayed and frozen on the screen. They should not tell anyone where they are on the map but use their knowledge of the language they have learned in the last three lessons to write directions, which they then text in using ActivExpression. All of the responses are then seeded to the screen and the "Who answered what list" is pasted to the screen.

The teacher now selects the directions sent in, one pair at a time, and all the other students discuss the directions and work out where they think that pair has ended up on the map.

Then, using the text function, they send in their solutions in French (or the language being studied). The pair of students whose turn it is now come out to the front and, pointing with their fingers to the map, give their directions in spoken French. Everyone will now see if they were right.

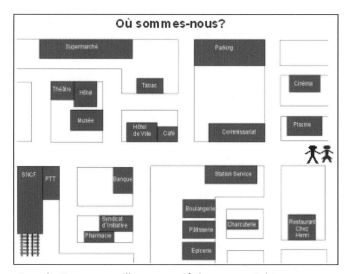

All the students will be involved in this and they will have to practice their writing skills in the texting phase of the activity, and their speaking skills when it is their turn to reveal the place on the map that they had chosen.

Thanks to Gail Lambert for the use of the map.

Jekyll and Hyde

Aims of the starter

This start to the lesson is designed to get the students interrogating the text from a novel, and what they find will be used to deepen understanding later in the lesson.

Target teaching group

Ages 14–16

Context

The class has been studying the novel and the teacher has selected an extract for interrogation. The passage is on the open page of the novel held by each student.

How does the lesson work?

Many students brought up on a diet of testing get used to scanning documents, looking for answers rather than studying them or reading them for deeper understanding. Effective tasks can force students to study information in more detail and, by using ActivExpression, teachers can monitor this process while at the same time motivating the students.

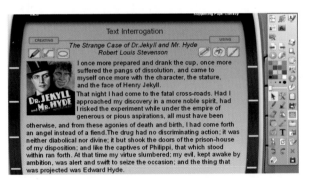

Working in pairs and discussing ideas before responding, students work their way through the Self-Paced questions, texting in responses when they are ready. The use of ActivExpression allows the teacher to monitor progress live and also to seed responses to the screen so that the whole class can be involved in analysis later.

Self-Paced questions in the activity are shown below.

The responses will be seeded to the screen when the teacher is ready to analyze the responses from the class. The whiteboard tools can be used for students to come out and highlight words, phrases, or passages. Differences in opinions can be debated.

	Question	Question Type	Level
1	What two word phrase shows that this is not the first occasion that this potion has been t...	Text	Level 1
2	Which word in the extract is a synonym for the word physique?	Multiple Choice	Level 1
3	Which word in the passage means fatal?	Text	Level 1
4	Which character prepared and drank from the cup at this point in the narrative	Multiple Choice	Level 1
5	What did Henry Jeckyll think about the drug he had discovered?	Multiple Choice	Level 1
6	What does Jekyll suggest may have happened if he had approached his discovery in a mo...	Multiple Choice	Level 1
7	What metaphor is used to descibe the effect of the drug on a persons disposition?	Text	Level 2
8	Which words in the passage show that the character transformation was painful	Text	Level 2

This activity makes use of an existing resource—the novel—but uses ActivExpression to generate the thinking, the discussion, and the considered responses. The real benefit comes when the responses are seeded and the teacher is able to ask students to justify responses or explain differences of opinion. The live feedback during the activity allows the teacher to intervene early if problems are identified.

Grateful thanks to the United Church Schools Trust in the UK for permission to adapt some flipchart pages from their forthcoming training materials "ActivExpression for Learning."

Stratovolcano

Aims of the starter
In the previous lesson, the class had been introduced to a Stratovolcano, and the teacher had explained the structure and features using a cross-sectional diagram. In this lesson, the topic will be explored further and the starting activity is to get the students to show what they can remember from the previous lesson.

Target teaching group
Ages 14–18

Context
The handsets are collected as students walk through the door. The interactive whiteboard screen has been frozen with the diagram on the right.

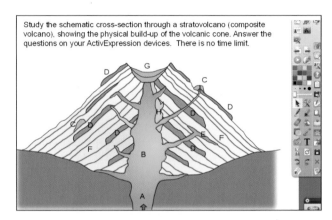

Study the schematic cross-section through a stratovolcano (composite volcano), showing the physical build-up of the volcanic cone. Answer the questions on your ActivExpression devices. There is no time limit.

The handsets have been registered with the hub and the Self-Paced activity has been activated by the teacher. As soon as each learner sits down and switches on ActivExpression, the questions begin. At this stage no names have been registered so responses are anonymous. The learners start answering the questions.

The questions
There are seven Self-Paced questions in the starter. The questions are set out below.

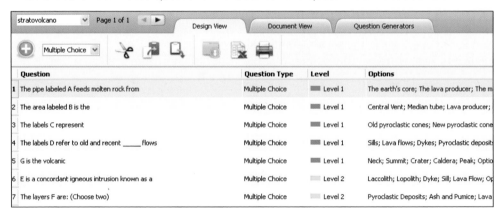

	Question	Question Type	Level	Options
1	The pipe labeled A feeds molten rock from	Multiple Choice	Level 1	The earth's core; The lava producer; The m
2	The area labeled B is the	Multiple Choice	Level 1	Central Vent; Median tube; Lava producer;
3	The labels C represent	Multiple Choice	Level 1	Old pyroclastic cones; New pyroclastic cone
4	The labels D refer to old and recent _____ flows	Multiple Choice	Level 1	Sills; Lava flows; Dykes; Pyroclastic deposit
5	G is the volcanic	Multiple Choice	Level 1	Neck; Summit; Crater; Caldera; Peak; Optio
6	E is a concordant igneous intrusion known as a	Multiple Choice	Level 2	Laccolith; Lopolith; Dyke; Sill; Lava Flow; O
7	The layers F are: (Choose two)	Multiple Choice	Level 2	Pyroclastic Deposits; Ash and Pumice; Lava

This starter linked with ongoing work, engaging learners with a task that required them to show what they had learned about the structure of a stratovolcano from the previous lesson. Once the activity is over, the teacher brings up the class list and PINs, and the handsets are registered with names. The data from this exercise will influence how much revision is needed with individuals or the whole class before moving onto further work on volcanoes.

Thanks to Pete Lambert from Promethean for this contribution.

Ending Lessons

In the Starting Lessons section, I explained the importance of "starting as you mean to go on," emphasizing that if teachers get the first few minutes of a lesson right then the learning that follows is likely to be more productive. The ending of lessons is equally as important. Why is this?

Firstly, one of the key characteristics of outstanding lessons is that all learners leave the lesson having made progress. Making lesson aims clear and ensuring that those aims are differentiated then becomes a prerequisite: How can you judge progress if you are not sure what you are trying to learn and how can everyone make progress if the aims are pitched too high or too low?

So, activities toward the end of the lesson should provide opportunities for all students to show how their knowledge, skill, or motivation has improved as a result of the learning experiences in the lesson. The assessment of progress at the end of a lesson therefore, and it doesn't have to be a test or formal assessment, must satisfy three key criteria. It must (1) involve all students, (2) be differentiated, and (3) be observable.

ActivExpression provides for all three of these criteria. Assessment of progress can, of course, be achieved through a formal or informal test, but it can also be done in more imaginative ways, engaging learners and ensuring that they leave the lesson (a) with "their heads held high" and (b) looking forward to the next lesson with you!

This Ending Lessons chapter will offer some examples of those kinds of activities.

"Try to ensure that students leave your room at the end of each lesson with their heads held high."

Guidance given to the author, Robert Powell,
on his first day in teaching in 1972.

En Ville Prepositions

Aims at the end of the lesson

In the previous lesson, the teacher introduced basic directions in French and this lesson is designed to add the use of prepositions such as "opposite," "next to," and "in front of." This end-of-lesson activity will allow the teacher to assess students' progress on this aspect of the language.

Target teaching group

This is targeted at 10–12-year-olds.

Context

Students have been taught and have practiced prepositions in the context of giving and receiving directions in a town.

How does the lesson work?

The teacher has prepared a second flipchart from the one used in lesson one. This one has a town map. Self-Paced questions in French have been prepared from Level 1 to Level 2. The flipchart is frozen on the screen and the Self-Paced mode begins.

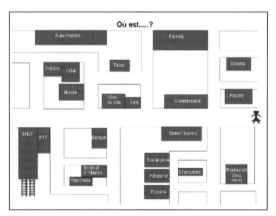

This idea of using an existing image and creating Self-Paced questions to go with it means that teachers of a foreign language might do this for family trees, shopping, transport, sports, and so on. Course books usually have excellent images and some of the questions can also be converted into Self-Paced.

Examples of the type of Self-Paced questions are below.

The assessment, which involves all the students, will inform the teacher what has been mastered and can be used to see which language elements need to be revised before the next "give us a clue" lesson.

	Question	Question Type	Level	Options	Correct Answers
1	L'hôtel est en face du théâtre.	Yes/No	Level 1	Yes; No	No
2	Le PTT est à côté du SNCF	Yes/No	Level 1	Yes; No	Yes
3	La station service est en face du co...	Yes/No	Level 1	Yes; No	Yes
4	Le tabac est derrière le café.	Yes/No	Level 1	Yes; No	No
5	La pâtisserie est .... la charcuter...	Text	Level 2		en face de
6	La pâtisserie est .... la boulange...	Text	Level 2		à côté de
7	Le supermarché est .... l' hôtel	Text	Level 2		en face de
8	Le musée est .... l' hôtel	Text	Level 2		avant

Thanks to Gail Lambert for this contribution.

Give Us A Clue

Aims at the end of the lesson

The teacher wants to assess the understanding of the lesson and also to develop the students' thinking skills.

Target teaching group

This idea of asking students to give clues for a person, an event, an object, an animal, a country, a character, a chemical, and so on can work in any lesson and with students of all ages. The "contestant" gets clues from the other students and the only rules are: (a) no speaking, (b) no gestures or mimes, (c) no use of the name of the object, person, etc. All the students can do is to text in a clue.

Context

This activity would be a good end to any lesson where the class has to use their knowledge from that lesson to give clues to the "contestants"; the more accurate the clues, the better the understanding. This activity can also be used for technical terms or definitions.

How does the lesson work?

The teacher chooses the first "contestant," who is blindfolded. The word or image is displayed to the rest of the class and then removed. A blank flipchart screen is displayed and the text function on Inspire is activated. Students think up a good clue and text it. (Self-Paced can also be used with the option to send in more than one clue.) The teacher now displays the results and seeds the clues to the screen. The contestant has 10 guesses from the clues to get the answer.

Examples of the types of words or images that might be the subjects for the clues are shown.

Only one word or image would be displayed at a time, but every time the contestant guesses correctly, she or he says which clue was the best and the person who sent it becomes the next contestant. It might last for 10 minutes or so and in that time, 3 or 4 contestants might have had a go.

If teachers choose the Self-Paced option, all that happens is they insert the same instruction a number of times. This allows students who text in quickly to have another go.

Once the Self-Paced is over, save the *results*, open the results browser and seed the results to the screen. The "contestant" has 10 guesses.

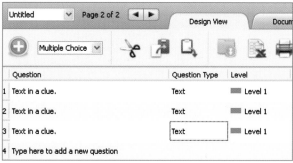

Fractions

Aims at the end of the lesson

To assess how well students can apply the concept of fractions in real life by asking them to walk around the room and find the photograph that represents the fraction they are seeking.

Target teaching group

This idea will work with any age.

Context

The class has been introduced to the concept of fractions and has practiced them through both whole-class questioning and short exercises from a Math book.

How does the lesson work?

The teacher has displayed 14 photographs labeled A to N on the classroom walls in different parts of the classroom. Self-Paced clues from Level 1 to Level 5 have been prepared and students are told to find the right photograph using their knowledge of fractions. Six of the 14 photographs are below to illustrate the idea of real-life fractions.

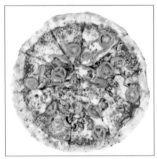

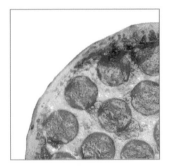

These should be placed in a random order in various parts of the classroom. If teachers would prefer not to have movement around the room, then the photographs can be arranged on a flipchart and the screen frozen when the Self-Paced starts. Teachers might also prefer to have photographs on a handout for each pair of students.

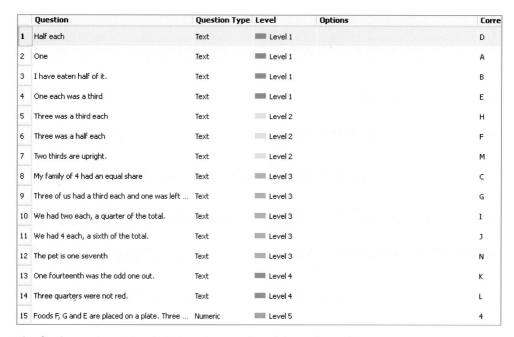

	Question	Question Type	Level	Options	Corre
1	Half each	Text	Level 1		D
2	One	Text	Level 1		A
3	I have eaten half of it.	Text	Level 1		B
4	One each was a third	Text	Level 1		E
5	Three was a third each	Text	Level 2		H
6	Three was a half each	Text	Level 2		F
7	Two thirds are upright.	Text	Level 2		M
8	My family of 4 had an equal share	Text	Level 3		C
9	Three of us had a third each and one was left …	Text	Level 3		G
10	We had two each, a quarter of the total.	Text	Level 3		I
11	We had 4 each, a sixth of the total.	Text	Level 3		J
12	The pet is one seventh	Text	Level 3		N
13	One fourteenth was the odd one out.	Text	Level 4		K
14	Three quarters were not red.	Text	Level 4		L
15	Foods F, G and E are placed on a plate. Three …	Numeric	Level 5		4

The final question, "*Foods F, G and E are placed on a plate. Three quarters are eaten, how many are left?*", is more challenging and requires a numeric response after doing a calculation.

This end to a lesson is likely to lead to engaged students at the time in a lesson when some may be losing interest. Teachers can make this as competitive as they wish, but some students will see it as a race to finish, whatever the teacher says.

Question Manager

In the Question Manager, the teacher has made two important selections.

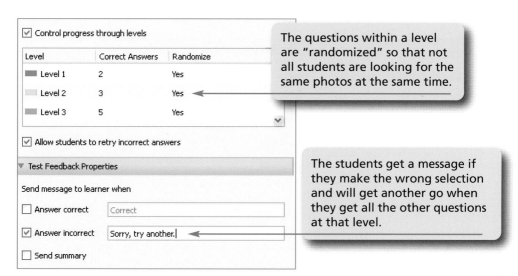

☑ Control progress through levels

Level	Correct Answers	Randomize
Level 1	2	Yes
Level 2	3	Yes
Level 3	5	Yes

☑ Allow students to retry incorrect answers

▼ Test Feedback Properties

Send message to learner when

☐ Answer correct   Correct

☑ Answer incorrect   Sorry, try another.

☐ Send summary

The questions within a level are "randomized" so that not all students are looking for the same photos at the same time.

The students get a message if they make the wrong selection and will get another go when they get all the other questions at that level.

The Wheel of Judgement

Aims at the end of the lesson

The teacher wants to encourage students to think logically in addressing moral and social issues, and to reinforce their understanding of the difference between evidence and value judgments.

Target teaching group

This concept of linking judgments to evidence can be developed in this way in most curriculum areas and with students of most ages.

Context

This activity would be a good end to any lesson where the class had been studying controversial issues, or examining scientific or sociological evidence on any number of topics. It might also be used for a class studying literature, seeking to make judgments about characters or motives, e.g. the motives of Shakespeare's Lady Macbeth.

How does the lesson work?

The teacher displays the "wheel of judgment" on the flipchart and then prepares a set of statements in Self-Paced format. Students have to select T, S, U, or V for each statement.

The wheel of judgment: The flipchart is frozen and the Self-Paced mode begins.

If teachers wish, the wheel of *judgment* can be copied and pasted to form new pages of the flipchart. The title is replaced by each of the statements.

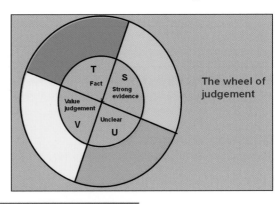

The wheel of judgement

Results showing the "who answered what list" can then be pasted to each page to aid discussion.

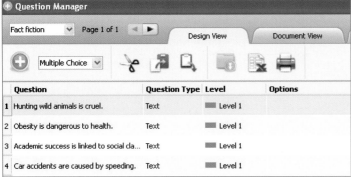

The results of the exercise are saved. The teacher then uses the *results* browser to view the responses from each statement in turn and pastes to the screen.

Question	Question Type	Level	Options
1 Hunting wild animals is cruel.	Text	Level 1	
2 Obesity is dangerous to health.	Text	Level 1	
3 Academic success is linked to social cla...	Text	Level 1	
4 Car accidents are caused by speeding.	Text	Level 1	

The introduction to the next lesson is now ready—a discussion on the results from the wheel of judgment exercise. Each statement and the responses will be shown and debated.

Aims at the end of the lesson

The class has just finished reading Of Mice and Men. The teacher tells them that for homework they will have to plan a piece of writing based on a critic's review of the novel in a serious newspaper or magazine. They will have to complete the writing under test conditions in the next lesson.

Target teaching group

This is targeted at students aged 14-16.

Context

The students have read the novel and throughout there have been discussions of the characters, the plot, the themes and the literary techniques used by Steinbeck.

How does the lesson work?

The teacher explains the review task for the next lesson and then opens a flipchart with the title in the middle.

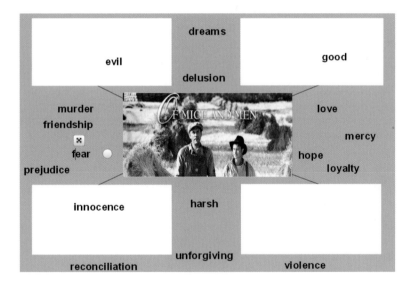

The teacher then gives all the students twenty seconds in silence to think of one key word or heading that might appear in their review.

They then have one minute in pairs to share their words and between them think of two more words. They are then asked to use ActivExpression in Self-Paced mode to text in their words. The same instruction in Self-Paced says 'text in your key word' and this is repeated up to 4 times. The teacher then saves the results, opens the results browser and seeds the words to the screen. The screen is printed and the students leave with an ideas poster to help their planning in homework.

Two-step Equations

Aims at the end of the lesson

The teacher has students with a wide range of skills in the class and wants to assess the understanding of two-step equations in order to plan the next lesson to meet the needs of the group.

Target teaching group

This is targeted at 13-year-olds.

Context

The teacher has introduced the topic of solving two-step equations. Several practice problems and examples have been completed. The teacher has prepared a Self-Paced question set for use at the end of the lesson to assess the understanding of solving two-step equations.

Question	Level
What is the first step in solving the equation $6x + 8 = 32$?	1
Solve the equation $5x + 2 = 17$	1
Solve $8x - 15 = 1$	1
Solve the equation $x/2 + 3 = 11$	1
Solve the equation $12x - 3x = 54$	1
$9x + 23 = 5$	2
Solve $x/3 - 8 = -4$	2
Solve the equation $-9 = 11x - 8x$	2
$1.3x - 2.5 = 1.4$	2
Solve the equation $-9x + 2x = -28$	2
Solve the equation $32 = 17 - x$	3
Solve the equation $x/-5 - 8 = -14$	3
Solve the equation $7 + 2/3x = -1$	3
Solve the equation $x/5 + 10 = 4/5$	3
A gym offers spinning classes for $10 per class and sells spinnin...	4
Your classroom has a $10,000 grant to buy technology equipm...	4
Find the error in solving the equation. $5 - 3x = 10$	4

How does the lesson work?

The questions are differentiated from Level 1 to Level 4. The Self-Paced session starts and the teacher monitors the computer screen in order to intervene with students who are struggling with the concept. The teacher can then make individual contact with the students as they work through the questions.

How can the data from the questions be subsequently used?

The data from the Self-Paced questions can be used for formative assessment. It enables the teacher to plan accordingly for the next class, knowing which students need greater challenge and which require support.

How does this help?

The live feedback from students is valuable to the teacher. The teacher is able to target support where it is needed and then make plans to work with students immediately or in the next lesson. It also provides specific information about where students are excelling, which helps the teacher to plan appropriate tasks and activities for these students in time for the next lesson. This kind of personalized intervention means that students are much more engaged with the lesson and feel more connected to their learning.

The use of ActivExpression in Self-Paced mode improves concentration and motivation, and the early intervention prevents students going too far with incorrect answers. If the teacher selects the "allow students to retry incorrect answers" option then a silly mistake the first time can be corrected, and the learner's confidence is not unduly damaged.

Finally, this type of assessment at the end of a lesson can provide valuable information if the teacher wants to differentiate in the setting of homework tasks.

Thanks to Amy Mallory, Greater Latrobe School District, Pennsylvania, for this contribution.

Case Studies

In the introduction to this book I emphasized that in looking closely at the impact that ActivExpression can have on the motivation, engagement, pace, participation, and monitoring of learners, I would include testimony from both teachers and students. This chapter contains descriptions of a series of real lessons from schools in the USA and the UK. The teachers who kindly allowed me to use these contributions are, without exception, modest individuals who will not claim that their ideas are "the best."

Indeed, there may be readers who are using ActivExpression in exciting and stimulating ways who feel that their lessons might have been featured in this book, and for them that opportunity will come if they read the final chapter, "*The Future.*"

These "case study" contributions do demonstrate, however, how many unsung heroes there are in our schools. As a former Principal of a High School, I would have been proud to have teachers like these working as partners and colleagues in the journey we are all on to make our schools and classrooms beacons of excellence.

The case studies are not organized into age or subject categories, although there are examples from many subject areas and from classes aged 5 to 18. The reason is simple. The vast majority of lesson plans in this chapter are transferable; the example might be for 5-year-olds in Math, but the same idea could be used with 12-year-olds in Spanish or 18-year-olds in Social Studies. The only ingredient needed is a degree of imagination!

Cha Cha Multiplication

"ActivExpression is my voice so I can tell people how smart I am. It makes me want to learn more because it is fun."

Student in the Cha-Cha Multiplication class

The challenge

Many learners grow up phobic about Math, particularly if they find it difficult. Teachers sometimes find ingenious ways to remove the fear and improve skills while making it fun.

Aims of the lesson

In this example, students practice their multiplication facts using ActivExpression accompanied by music and dance.

Target teaching group

Ages 8–11. Students of all abilities can participate.

Context

The teacher has discussed the importance of how knowing your multiplication facts makes more difficult math concepts possible. He has prepared a set of Self-Paced questions to practice and then assess the degree of knowledge of multiplication facts 1–12.

The questions

There were 30 Self-Paced questions in the set. A selection is shown below.

	Question	Question Type	Level	Options	Correct Ans
1	4 x 2	Numeric	Level 1		8
2	1 x 9	Numeric	Level 1		9
3	6 x 1	Numeric	Level 1		6
4	10 x 4	Numeric	Level 1		40
5	2 x 7	Numeric	Level 1		14
6	6 x 10	Numeric	Level 1		60
7	4 x 5	Numeric	Level 1		20
8	8 x 8	Numeric	Level 1		64
9	12 x 12	Numeric	Level 1		144
10	5 x 3	Numeric	Level 1		15
11	9 x 6	Numeric	Level 1		54

The questions were generated through the Self-Paced question-set wizard. All questions were set at Level 1 and randomized, incorrect answers were not allowed to be corrected, and a desired time limit was set.

The same idea might have been differentiated for other classes with more challenging questions, but the idea was to complete all 30 within the 3 minutes of the Cha-Cha dance. In this situation, the key purpose was to get all learners fluent in their multiplication tables.

60

Cha Cha Multiplication

How the lesson progressed

The Self-Paced questions started at the same time as the music/dance. As students were dancing and answering, the teacher used the live feedback to get an idea of how students were progressing.

This allowed him to spot those who were more focused on the dancing than the questions. He warned these students that if progress was not being made, then they would forfeit the right to participate in future "Cha-cha Slide Multiplication." That solved the problem!

How the data from the Self-Paced session was subsequently used

The data from the activity was used to determine who would need extra practice during Math workshops as well as help them prepare for the quarterly fluency test. Students that struggled with the activity were pulled into smaller groups to work on fluency. Learners kept track of their results in their Math notebook and noted the multiplication facts that were giving them difficulty, e.g. 8s or 9s. This information was given to them by the teacher through the live feedback.

The teacher's evaluation of the lesson

- We were trying to create a classroom environment that got students excited about their learning. Despite flash cards, timed tests, and other activities, we still had too many students struggling with the basic facts.
- When the idea of movement and music was brought up during collaboration with colleagues John Guyre and Savanna Green in our District, we decided to think outside the box. What has transpired since then has been nothing short of amazing.
- The live feedback of ActivExpression has revolutionized instruction in the classroom. With real-time updates, teachers are able to make immediate adjustments to the lesson or intervene with individual students to get the most out of valuable class time.
- Students were excited and motivated because they have never done Math computation with Math facts through music and movement.
- Computational fluency has soared to over 95% success rate among grade levels from a starting point of between 50% and 60%.

The students' evaluation of the lesson

- ActivExpression helps me learn because I can find out right away if I got the right answer or not. I can also find out what I need to do to fix it.
- It helps me concentrate more because I know I will get feedback on my answer immediately.
- ActivExpression allows everyone in the class to participate and be represented fairly.
- The music makes it fun so you are encouraged to do well.
- The beat of the music keeps me at a good pace as I answer the math problems.
- The music and ActivExpression make learning your math facts fun.

Thanks to Luke Dix, Cold Water Elementary School, Florissant, Missouri, for this contribution.

BODMAS

"I really like how I can move onto harder questions without having to wait for others in the class. It keeps my brain in gear."

11-year-old student

The challenge

Peanuts cartoon: "I've taught my dog to whistle." "I haven't heard it whistling." "I said I had taught it, not that it had learned." Good teaching always includes the process of consolidation..

Aims of the lesson

To consolidate understanding of the BODMAS rules for the order in which calculations are done: Brackets, Order, Division, Multiplication, Addition, and Subtraction.

Target teaching group

This is a group of 11-year-old students with a wide range of skills' levels.

Context

The teacher has introduced the topic and taught the class the BODMAS rules. She has prepared a set of Self-Paced questions both to assess and to consolidate the learners' understanding of the rules.

The questions

The actual set had 24 questions with 4 or 5 at each level. The image shows just a selection of these. The questions are differentiated with the rules on BODMAS appearing in the Level 3 questions and above. Some of the more skilled students would move through to Level 5 quite quickly.

	Question	Question Type	Level	Options	Correct Answers
1	$3 + 5$	Numeric	Level 1		8
2	$9 + 1$	Numeric	Level 1		10
3	$14 + 15$	Numeric	Level 2		29
4	$17 + 11$	Numeric	Level 2		28
5	$3 + 2 \times 6$	Numeric	Level 3		15
6	$7 \times 2 + 11$	Numeric	Level 3		25
7	$2 \times (3 + 8)$	Numeric	Level 4		22
8	$(3 + 4) \times 2$	Numeric	Level 4		14
9	$(4 + 3) + (5 - 2) \times 2$	Numeric	Level 5		13
10	$(2 \times 3) + 12 (10-8)$	Numeric	Level 5		30

The image also shows: Multiple Choice dropdown

The options chosen in the Question Master are set out here.

The students were able to progress to harder questions after getting two answers correct and were also allowed to retry incorrect answers.

☑ Control progress through levels

Level	Correct Answers	Randomize
Level 1	2	No
Level 2	2	No
Level 3	2	No

☑ Allow students to retry incorrect answers

How the lesson progressed

The Self-Paced session started and the teacher monitored the progress on the computer screen. It was evident from the live feedback screen that the students were comfortable with the early Level 1 and Level 2 questions, even though some learners were taking longer than others to complete their calculations. Mistakes began to show on the feedback screen as soon as some learners started on Level 3 questions.

A number of issues were identified:
- Some learners had forgotten the BODMAS rules and for question 7 were giving the answer "30" instead of the correct answer of "15" because they were performing the addition before the multiplication.
- Some students, for question 9, followed the sequence of tasks as the question is set out and responded with an answer of "66" instead of performing both multiplications before the addition to achieve the correct answer of "26."

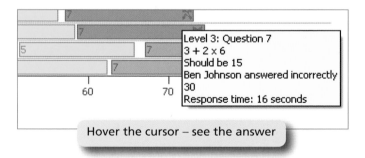

Level 3: Question 7
$3 + 2 \times 6$
Should be 15
Ben Johnson answered incorrectly
30
Response time: 16 seconds

Hover the cursor – see the answer

Intervention

The live feedback from the computer screen on the progress of all learners enabled a number of interventions to take place:
- As soon as mistakes were highlighted on the feedback bar graph, both the teacher and the classroom assistant were able to move around the classroom to the learners concerned and remind them of the rules.
- The bar graph here shows that one student had obviously given up and was entering answers randomly without thought. The teacher was able to intervene.

- Some students called for help as soon as they received the "sorry, incorrect answer" message because they were confused. After this, they were able to proceed more confidently.
- The feedback told the teacher that lots of learners were struggling with questions 13 and 14 so the Self-Paced activity was paused and the teacher spent a few minutes with the whole class, working through the problem to help them remember the rules.

The teacher's evaluation of the lesson

There were a number of important issues that emerged from the use of ActivExpression in this lesson:

- I did not realise how many learners were wasting time in previous lessons when we worked through these problems on the whiteboard as a whole class. Those who understood it first time were waiting for others to catch up.
- Some learners in the past, when working on paper, would make the same mistake in a whole string of questions, because in a large class I would not get around the room quickly enough to spot the errors being made.

The students' evaluation of the lesson

- I really enjoy using ActivExpression because it tells me when I make a mistake and I can correct it. I like getting the answers right, even if it takes a few goes.
- I like Math so get frustrated when I know the answer, I put my hand up but the teacher doesn't pick me. With ActivExpression I get my answer in quickly and then get another question. It keeps me interested.
- It's cool. I find writing difficult and it takes me quite a long time to do the questions in my book. With ActivExpression I get things done quicker.

Thanks to Accrington Academy in Lancashire, UK, for this contribution.

Graphing Quadratic Functions

"I feel really prepared for my unit test! Using the ActivExpression was like completing a study guide with your teacher right beside you. When I got something wrong, I knew that instant. I had to go back and really take a look at my mistake before I could move on."

A student from this class

The challenge

Preparing for high-stakes unit tests is very important to students and teachers. Sometimes such sessions, working through worksheets or listening to the teacher going over key points, can be monotonous and dry, but not this lesson!

Aims of the lesson

To demonstrate an understanding of how the values a, b, and c of a given quadratic function in standard form affect the shape of its graph.

Target teaching group

This lesson is for any students taking Algebra I or Algebra II with a clear understanding of graphing quadratic functions.

Context

The teacher has introduced the parent quadratic function and the standard form of a quadratic function: $ax^2 + bx + c$. The class has also discussed how the values of a, b, and c change the shape of a parabola and have graphed a variety of parabolas by hand. She has prepared a set of Self-Paced questions to assess the degree of understanding the students have on the connection between a given quadratic function and its graph.

The questions

There were 18 Self-Paced instructions or questions in the set. The questions, type of questions, and levels are shown below.

Graphing Quadratic Functions

The class was an advanced math class organized into pairs of students and it was made clear that they were competing with other pairs.

	Question	Question Type	Level	Optio
3	x^2 - 3	Text	■ Level 1	
4	x^2 - 7x + 10	Text	Level 2	
5	- x^2 - 2x + 1	Text	Level 2	
6	- x^2 - 2x - 1	Text	Level 3	
7	x^2 - 3x -5	Text	Level 3	
8	- 3x^2 - x + 2	Text	■ Level 4	
9	- x^2 + 3x - 2	Text	■ Level 4	
10	1/3 x^2 - 4	Text	Level 5	
11	3x^2 + 4	Text	Level 5	
12	-3x^2 + 4	Text	■ Level 6	
13	-1/3 x^2 - 3	Text	■ Level 6	
14	1/4 x^2 - 3	Text	■ Level 7	
15	2x^2 + x -3	Text	■ Level 7	
16	x^2 - 2x - 3	Text	Level 8	
17	x^2 + 2x - 3	Text	Level 8	
18	4x^2 + 3	Text	Level 8	
19	-x^2 - 2x + 3	Text	Level 9	

All the questions in the Self-Paced set asked students to text in which algebra question matched which graph. Each pair of students had a set of 18 graphs labeled alphabetically and their task was to send in the right letter to match the algebra and the graph. (Although these graphs were on paper, they might have been placed on the whiteboard as a set of graphs with the screen frozen.)

Two of the 18 graphs are below to illustrate the kind of challenge students faced.

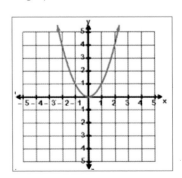 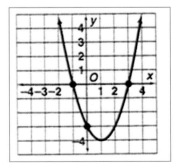

How the lesson progressed

The Self-Paced session started and I monitored the progress on the computer screen. I was able to clearly see which students understood how the values of a, b, and c changed the graph of the quadratic function. As the questions increased in difficulty, I was able to monitor the exact amount of time it took for students to get a particular question correct. I was also able to see which variable students tended to struggle with most.

The teacher's evaluation of the lesson

- The students were highly engaged. They thoroughly enjoyed moving at a pace that they found comfortable. As a teacher, it was extremely easy for me to assess which students had a clear understanding and where students were struggling.
- I was also able to see the amount of time it took for students to answer each question.
- For this particular activity, I let the students work in teams of two. The math conversations I heard around the room were extremely rich.
- Students were not allowed to use any paper or a pencil, so it was interesting to hear their different strategies and thought processes.
- Since the lesson was Self-Paced, there was also an added bonus of healthy competition. Students were constantly glancing at the screen to see what level they were on, as well as their classmates. At the end, the energy was high as three teams battled for a first-place finish!

The students' evaluation of the lesson

- I knew my team needed a strategy. I looked at the board and saw that our bar was yellow, when most groups' bars were orange! We stopped and strategized. After that, we were on a roll!
- It was like playing a game on my cell phone! I had to know my math, but I also had to know how to text quickly!
- I feel really prepared for my unit test! Using the ActivExpression was like completing a study guide with your teacher right beside you. When I got something wrong, I knew that instant. I had to go back and really take a look at my mistake before I could move on.

Thanks to Lakesha Goff, Ron Clark Academy, Atlanta, Georgia.

Cause and Effect

"This lesson was fun for me as the teacher because it took a boring drill-type worksheet and turned it into an interactive and engaging lesson."

The teacher in this lesson

The challenge

All learners must master the basic skills, including reading and comprehension, if they are to be successful in their learning in later years. Sometimes, tasks aimed at developing these skills can become boring and dry. In this lesson the teacher planned an engaging lesson that practiced these skills in a fun way.

Aims of the lesson

To get students to practice and use their reading and comprehension skills accurately in order to identify causes with their corresponding effects.

Target teaching group

Grades 4–5, ages 9–11

Context

This lesson served as practice, using reading to identify cause and effect. Prior to this lesson, the class had read together multiple stories, identified cause/effect relationships throughout, and written down various effects given a cause and various causes given an effect.

The questions

This lesson began with a review of what we had learned about cause and effect and how we identify those relationships. A flipchart page with a list of "effects" is opened on the screen.

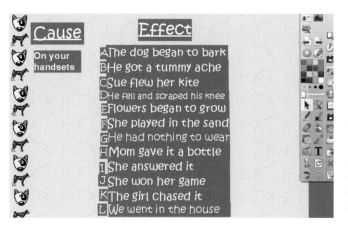

A list of causes has been prepared in Self-Paced format on the handsets, all at Level 1. The option to report wrong answers was selected with the words "sorry, try again."

	Question	Question Type	Level	Options	Correct Answers
1	Grandma plants seeds	Text	Level 1		E
2	It was raining outside	Text	Level 1		L
3	The phone rang	Text	Level 1		I
4	The baby began to cry	Text	Level 1		H
5	The butterfly is pretty	Text	Level 1		K
6	Someone came to the door	Text	Level 1		A
7	It is a windy day	Text	Level 1		C
8	The boy ran too fast	Text	Level 1		D
9	Billy ate too many cookies	Text	Level 1		B
10	The girl practiced hard	Text	Level 1		J
11	All the clothes were dirty	Text	Level 1		G
12	Sam got her a shovel and pail	Text	Level 1		F

The Self-Paced session begins and students are presented with a series of short "causes" from the list above. They have to decide which of the "effects" is the likely match and then text in the appropriate letter, e.g. "A," "B," and so on. This activity tests their reading, their understanding, and their skills of reasoning.

How the lesson progressed
The students completed the activity in almost total silence, some reading to themselves as they worked out the right "effect."

Some students, eager to be "the first," made choices too quickly and were told by the handset response to have another try. Some began to argue that their "wrong" answer did make sense. The bar graphs for each student showed that many took a long time to answer in order to make sure that they chose the right one, and this was a very useful lesson in why it is sometimes a good idea to weigh up decisions rather than rushing in with the first answer that comes into your head.

We then revealed the results on the screen. We took each "cause" in turn and it was interesting how some students who had made an original "wrong" answer justified their choices:

> *"When the phone rings in my house, the dog does begin to bark!"*

There was a series of quite heated debates on some of the causes/effects and students were very eager to defend their own choices, although this one was not accepted by the rest of the class:

> *"He fell and scraped his knee because he had eaten too many cookies
> and was overweight!"*

Cause and Effect

How the feedback was used

It was obvious from the feedback that the majority of the class had been able accurately to read and understand the statements, and their choices were made with sound understanding. Some, however, found the logical decisions and the reading difficult, so the data enabled further support to be targeted.

The teacher's evaluation of the lesson
- This lesson was really enjoyable and full of student interaction. Because of the high levels of engagement, the discussions amongst my students were at deeper levels than normal and yielded really positive results.
- ActivExpression worked really well. When they were making their choices in Self-Paced mode, the levels of concentration and motivation were amazing and the desire to get answers right was widespread.
- I found the live monitoring very useful with some learners obviously valuing speed over accuracy! I was able to intervene here quite quickly.
- The facility to send a "sorry, try again" message was invaluable, making students much more careful over subsequent questions.
- The assessment of "wrong" sent by ActivExpression to each learner is private and I know that it reduces the anxiety that some weaker students feel when this is public.

The students' evaluation of the lesson
- We love using ActivExpression. We always groan whenever our teacher says "no handsets are needed today."
- When one our friends sends in a wrong answer, we want to know why to see if we can help.
- When I make a mistake using ActivExpression, it tells me. I like that better than being told in front of the class.
- I don't feel worried if I get something wrong using ActivExpression. I know I can have another go at getting it right.

Thanks to Savanna Green from Lawson Elementary School, Hazelwood School District, Florissant, Missouri.

"With ActivExpression I loved trying to beat my buddies. It's much more exciting than tests or worksheets!"

A student from this class

The challenge

Teachers are sometimes faced with long lessons, on a difficult topic, with a group of students whose skills vary quite markedly.

Aims of the lesson

To consolidate the learning on converging lenses and apply what they have learned to the creation of refracting telescopes, calculating magnification for a variety of lens combinations.

Target teaching group

This was a group of 16-year-olds facing their end of High School examinations. The group had students who would achieve top grades and those that might score a pass.

Context

The students had been introduced to the key foundation knowledge for this topic and they would take it further in this lesson. Three sets of Self-Paced questions had been prepared: (1) to do a quick test on the previous learning, (2) to assess new learning from this lesson, and (3) a final one to assess students on the whole of the topic.

The Learning Cycle

The teacher likes to use the theory of the "Learning Cycle."

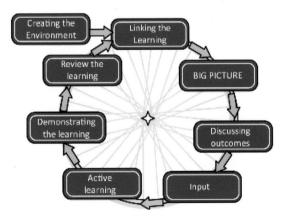

This theory, based on the work of Alistair Smith in the UK, suggests the following cycle:

1. Link the learning
2. Give the big picture
3. Discuss outcomes
4. Input
5. Active learning
6. Demonstrate the learning
7. Review the learning

The teacher built this "cycle" into the way the lesson was planned, using ActivExpression as a central resource in the delivery.

How the lesson progressed

Phase 1: Linking the learning. What can you remember from last lesson?
A set of Self-Paced questions was prepared to encourage recall from the previous lesson.
Examples. There were several questions for each Level—this just shows one of each.

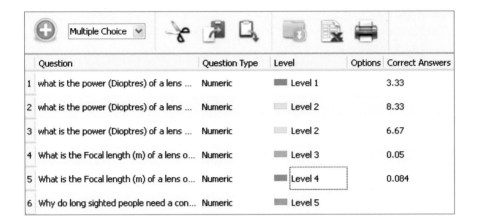

	Question	Question Type	Level	Options	Correct Answers
1	what is the power (Dioptres) of a lens ...	Numeric	Level 1		3.33
2	what is the power (Dioptres) of a lens ...	Numeric	Level 2		8.33
3	what is the power (Dioptres) of a lens ...	Numeric	Level 2		6.67
4	What is the Focal length (m) of a lens o...	Numeric	Level 3		0.05
5	What is the Focal length (m) of a lens o...	Numeric	Level 4		0.084
6	Why do long sighted people need a con...	Numeric	Level 5		

This Self-Paced activity was done on entry to the room—very little introduction—
providing a fast and focused start to the lesson.

It soon became clear that several of the students had misconceptions from the previous
lesson. The teacher was able to move quickly to them and question them to discover the
misconception. Immediately all the students could access the Level 1 questions.

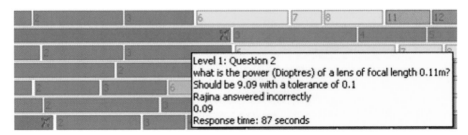

Level 1: Question 2
what is the power (Dioptres) of a lens of focal length 0.11m?
Should be 9.09 with a tolerance of 0.1
Rajina answered incorrectly
0.09
Response time: 87 seconds

However, once the class reached the Level 2 questions they found they were all
struggling as the questions now were giving focal length in centimeters, where it need to
be in meters to calculate power.

The dynamic feedback allowed the teacher to pause the questions and help the class to
see where they were going wrong.

They were able to retry incorrect answers and all students progressed to Level 3.

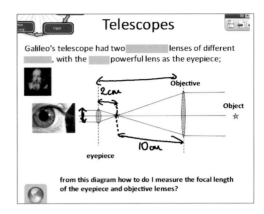

The role of ActivExpression was critical here. In this phase of the lesson, the teacher was able to identify a major problem that he had not anticipated—the live feedback instantly alerted him and he was able to change the lesson plan to meet students' needs.

Question	Question Type	Level	Opt	Corre
1 What si the magnification with a telescope eyepiece FL=4cm, objective FL=15	Numeric	Level 1		3.75
2 what eyepiece FL do you need for a magnification of X20 with an objective lens of 100cm	Numeric	Level 2		5
3 what eyepiece FL do you need for a magnification of X20 with an objective lens of 16cm	Numeric	Level 2		0.8
4 If you were given a box of random converging lenses how would you make select lense...	Text	Level 3		
5 Type here to add a new question				

How the lesson continued.

Phase 4: Input. The teacher then introduced the students to the new learning on Telescopes, which involved interaction and discussion and then another Self-Paced assessment. (Only a selection of questions from each level has been set out above.)

Phase 5 of the lesson took the students further into the use of mirrors and lenses, and in Phase 6 they had to make predictions based on their new learning. In Phase 7 a third set of Self-Paced questions reviewed their understanding of the whole unit of work.

The teacher's evaluation of the lesson
- The opening assessment only took slightly less than 10 minutes and allowed me to accurately link the learning into this lesson. This was a much more efficient and evidence-based way to move forwards within a lesson sequence.
- With ActivExpression, assessments are so easy to administer and analyze it enabled me to move through the phases with confidence that I had not "lost" anyone.
- The two-hour lesson passed very quickly—the pace was maintained throughout and so was the motivation of the students.

The students' evaluation of the lesson
- I hated it when I was getting the questions wrong; when I found out what silly mistakes I was making with units, I was able to fly through.
- It means I don't have to wait for others so I can go much faster than I've been able to before.

Thanks to Ben Cobbold, Swindon Academy, UK, for this contribution.

"As soon as we hit the green button, they are off to the races and completely zoned in. It's the same as getting the results to the test, but you can see everyone's progress in live time."

The teacher for this class

The challenge

Many learners are not good at listening to instructions, relying on their friends to explain later. In a practical science lesson, this is a real problem. This teacher uses ActivExpression to provide instructions, questions, and challenges in a science practical.

Aims of the lesson

I am using the ActivExpression in this activity to force students to read and follow simple directions. The focus of the lesson was to demonstrate Newton's 3rd law of motion.

Target teaching group

Grade 8 (ages 13–14.) However, it can be applied for use in any lab where students have to follow simple instructions.

Context

Prior to the activity, we reviewed Newton's Laws of Motion and observed many examples of the applications of the laws.

The instructions and questions

There were nine Self-Paced instructions or questions in the set, a mixture of multiple choice and text, from Level 1 to Level 8.

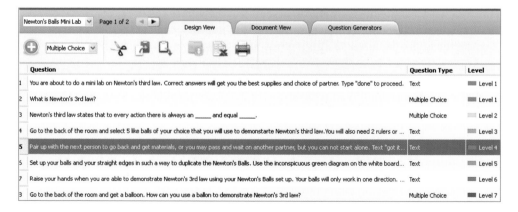

Some of the instructions were quite long; some gave clues. Two are reproduced below.

Commentary

Go to the back of the room and select 5 like balls of your choice that you will use to demonstrate Newton's third law. You will also need 2 rulers or other straight edges. Return to your seat and type "done" after you have selected your balls and straight edges.

Commentary

Set up your balls and your straight edges in such a way to duplicate the Newton's Balls. Use the inconspicuous green diagram on the white board as a hint. Text "u slick Mr. T" when you have completed your set-up.

How the lesson progressed

The lab progressed just as planned. The faster, more accurate students got their choice of partners. Labs are 20% of the grade so it helps to work with someone who will work as hard to get the tasks done correctly.

This activity only took about 20 minutes, but before the use of ActivExpression for giving the directions, similar activities have taken much longer.

Students had to text specified responses once they achieved, or thought they achieved, certain tasks. I would instruct them to proceed, but only if they had followed the directions. With no diagrams to help and few oral directions, the students were able to proceed quietly through the lab to the finished product.

How the data from the Self-Paced session was subsequently used

The data was used two-fold. The students were evaluated first on their reading and comprehension skills. Too often they rely on photos, classmates, and/or oral interpretation of very simple tasks. This type of activity builds self-confidence as students succeed. Secondly, the students were able to practice and apply Newton's 3rd law. Each lab has its own set of materials and procedures. Students have learned that they must at the least take a mental note while proceeding through such activities because a formal lab report of the results must be submitted within a couple of days. So when constructing my procedures, I keep them as simple as possible to give the students a chance at recalling them later in the class period.

The teacher's evaluation of the lesson

- ActivExpression has added a new dimension to my classroom. The labs have not changed, but ActivExpression has revolutionized them. The students are more focused and work much more quietly while anticipating the final product.
- From a pop in a test tube from igniting hydrogen gas given off from the reaction of magnesium and hydrochloric acid, to releasing a balloon across the classroom, the students rarely know what the surprise will be in the end. They know that they will see it only if they follow the directions on the ActivExpression.
- I can monitor both on the screen and at the students' work area. The live data allows me to anticipate mistakes in the tough areas and be on the spot as students proceed, and the pacing is literally my GPS around the classroom.
- When the students begin to text answers, the classroom atmosphere is equivalent only to that of a final exam as students totally focus on the questions streaming through on the ActivExpression screen. The excitement builds as each level is achieved. By the end of the activity, there is a buzz of excitement and a sense of accomplishment.

The students' evaluation of the lesson

- I love the challenge of reading the instructions while competing with others in the class to complete the tasks.
- When we use ActivExpression, we like the anticipation of seeing what the next step is and pay close attention to the detail to make sure we follow the steps correctly.
- I like looking at the data at the end—we debate the responses.
- We are very competitive so don't waste a second of time working in this way. If we wasted any time, it would affect our finishing positions.
- It is easy to hide in whole-class questioning if we don't know. There is nowhere to hide on the ActivExpression. The teacher can see every answer given.

Thanks to Ken Townsel, Ron Clark Academy, Atlanta, Georgia.

"I will never forget one extremely timid student who always seemed to have his head on the desk. The one thing that never failed to engage him was putting an ActivExpression handset in his hands."

The teacher for this class

The challenge

Teachers of older students (16+) often struggle to get them to participate actively in lessons. Many learners expect the teacher to provide notes/information which they file away for later.

Aims of the lesson

1. To demonstrate the power and influence the media has on the voting public in Democracies.
2. To evaluate media bias and determine its effectiveness in politics.

Target teaching group

This lesson was created for Advanced Placement 10th-graders on a United States Government and Politics Course.

Context

Students have been studying the history of the media and its role in government, politics, and elections. A key concept that had been previously discussed is narrowcasting (broadcasting news programs created for an audience of like ideologies).

How the lesson was planned

The teacher has embedded into the flipchart a series of broadcasts focusing on the first 100 days of Barack Obama's presidency. ActivExpression had been set up in Self-Paced mode using the Likert scale function, where students would be asked at various points of the speeches to log, on a 7-point scale, a response from "strongly disagree" to "strongly agree."

The first broadcast was President Obama himself, and the topics for his speech are shown on the flipchart below. As he covered each point, e.g. Iraq, students were prompted to vote on the 7-point scale to register degrees of agreement or disagreement on what he said on that issue.

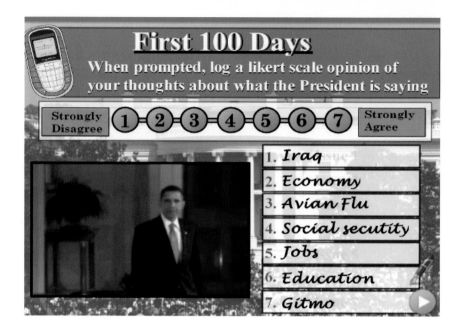

The results were saved and labeled Issue 1, Issue 2, Issue 3, and so on. The opinions, results, and data would be used later in the lesson.

How the lesson progressed

The second video was CNN's coverage of the aforementioned press conference. In the "news" coverage video, a liberal and conservative discuss their opinions of the press conference.

After the commentators gave their analysis, students were asked to log in their opinions about the President and his policies. During the video, area camera shots were taken by pressing the camera icon on the video playback bar. These images were resized and placed in the spaces provided to record moments when students' opinions were called for.

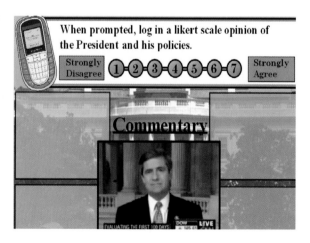

How the data from the Self-Paced session was subsequently used

In addition to real-time use, the data was first exported to Excel, averaged, and finally graphed. In the data from the first video, students were able to clearly see which of the President's policies were most important to them. In reviewing the data, "college loans" and "jobs" caused student responses to spike towards the "strongly agree" side of the

Likert scale. This data was used as a springboard to a discussion about how the President must tailor his words to his audiences.

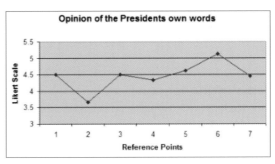

The final, critical part of the lesson was the data from the second video. After listening to a liberal speak about the President and his policies, the students were more likely to agree with the President and his policies; while after listening to a conservative pundit, the students were more likely to disagree with the President and his policies. This data led to vibrant discussions on the role of the media and how narrowcasting to audiences causes political polarization instead of moderation.

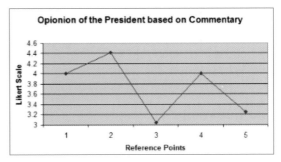

The teacher's evaluation of the lesson

- It was really an "aha" moment. The use of ActivExpression dramatically increased the engagement of the students while watching the video, and the discussion after was more intense and inclusive than ever before.
- I have been asked by other teachers about ActivExpression and a question that often comes up is: "Does asking students to text in their responses limit the depth of discussion in your classroom?" The truth is that it DEEPENS the conversations. The technology is the springboard.

The students' evaluation of the lesson

- I was surprised that we were able to answer questions continually during the video instead of the teacher having to pause the video to ask the questions.
- It was really interesting to see how much our opinions were influenced by the opinions of others.
- Having to vote at particular points of the video made me concentrate much more than in the past. You couldn't switch off for a second.
- The debate after the video was great. We all got involved.

Thanks to Timothy Short from Poolesville High School, Montgomery County Public Schools, Maryland, for this contribution.

Chunking Math

"This is so much more fun than those papers you give us."

Grade 1 student in this class

The challenge

Young children can often develop a phobia about Math if their early experiences are not good. In this lesson, the Grade 1 students find the learning of basic Math skills great fun.

Aims of the lesson

The students will use basic addition or subtraction rules (Doubles + 1, Minus 0, Minus 1, etc.) to compute mathematical problems.

Target teaching group

Grade 1 (5- and 6-year-olds).

Context

The teacher has introduced the mathematical rule being assessed, created a flipchart with Self-Paced questions that assess that rule, and taught students how to use the ActivExpression handsets to input answers.

The questions

After teaching the mathematical rule, the teacher opens the flipchart for the rule being taught. All questions are the same difficulty, Level 1, because of the chunking of the skill.

	Question	Question Type	Level	Options	Correct Answers
	Multiple Choice ⌄				
1	9 + 2	Numeric	Level 1		11
2	6 + 3	Numeric	Level 1		9
3	1 + 1	Numeric	Level 1		2
4	8 + 1	Numeric	Level 1		9
5	5 + 1	Numeric	Level 1		6
6	2 + 1	Numeric	Level 1		3
7	9 + 1	Numeric	Level 1		10
8	3 + 2	Numeric	Level 1		5
9	10 + 3	Numeric	Level 1		13
10	7 + 3	Numeric	Level 1		10
11	4 + 3	Numeric	Level 1		7

There were 100 questions in this Self-Paced set. Five minutes were given for the Self-Paced section of the lesson. Live scoring was used by the teacher only. Students were not shown results.

The children worked at different speeds, but all were practicing the rule.

How the data was used

Using the Self-Paced questions enabled the teacher to get immediate feedback of student mastery of the skill. By looking at the data, the teacher was able to determine who needed reinforcement and who was ready for enrichment. From the results, the teacher was able to form small groups and deliver future instruction based on the individual needs of each student.

The teacher's evaluation of the lesson

- I found live scoring an amazing tool that I can't live without! I don't have to guess or wait to grade papers to see who mastered the skill.
- Students were actively engaged and loved using the ActivExpression devices. They all worked at their own pace and everyone felt successful, no matter what questions they were able to get through.

The students' evaluation of the lesson

- This is so much more fun than those papers you give us.
- I enjoy using ActivExpression because it makes my brain think harder.

Thanks to Sandy Boyd, Baltimore County Public Schools, Maryland, for this contribution.

"It is a lot more fun than writing! I also like the way the teacher can see if you get a question wrong and are struggling, and can come over and help you straight away without having to put your hand up."

A student in this lesson

The challenge
Preparing for tests is a bit like going to the dentist—necessary but not something you look forward to. This teacher made test preparation effective but enjoyable.

Aims of the lesson
To prepare the students for their forthcoming national tests.

Target teaching group
This was a class of 10- and 11-year-olds with a range of Math skills.

Context
This activity was planned to be a consolidation lesson.

How does the lesson work?
A Self-Paced activity was created using a Carroll diagram as the focal point.

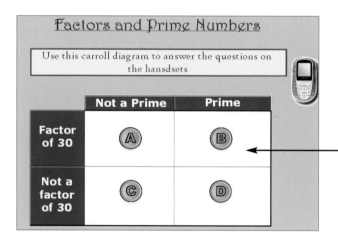

ommentary

This Carroll diagram was shown to the class and the teacher explained how it works. The screen was frozen and the Self-Paced activity began. The Carroll diagram can be used in a variety of contexts.

The questions
There were 22 questions in all, with a minimum of five questions at Levels 3 and 4.

- multiple choice
- yes/no
- number
- text

Some questions were open-ended.

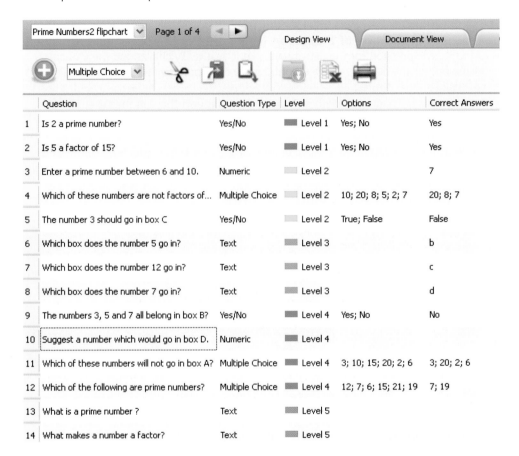

	Question	Question Type	Level	Options	Correct Answers
1	Is 2 a prime number?	Yes/No	Level 1	Yes; No	Yes
2	Is 5 a factor of 15?	Yes/No	Level 1	Yes; No	Yes
3	Enter a prime number between 6 and 10.	Numeric	Level 2		7
4	Which of these numbers are not factors of...	Multiple Choice	Level 2	10; 20; 8; 5; 2; 7	20; 8; 7
5	The number 3 should go in box C	Yes/No	Level 2	True; False	False
6	Which box does the number 5 go in?	Text	Level 3		b
7	Which box does the number 12 go in?	Text	Level 3		c
8	Which box does the number 7 go in?	Text	Level 3		d
9	The numbers 3, 5 and 7 all belong in box B?	Yes/No	Level 4	Yes; No	No
10	Suggest a number which would go in box D.	Numeric	Level 4		
11	Which of these numbers will not go in box A?	Multiple Choice	Level 4	3; 10; 15; 20; 2; 6	3; 20; 2; 6
12	Which of the following are prime numbers?	Multiple Choice	Level 4	12; 7; 6; 15; 21; 19	7; 19
13	What is a prime number ?	Text	Level 5		
14	What makes a number a factor?	Text	Level 5		

How the lesson progressed

The majority of children were able to answer the Level 1 questions quickly and progressed onto the Level 2 questions, with most children reaching the point of working their way through the Level 4 questions. One child was able to speed through the questions and reached the extension Level 5 questions!

Intervention

- Immediately the live answers showed that three students were answering incorrectly. It was possible to identify them straight away and to provide them with tailored support. One had forgotten that 1 and 2 were prime numbers and after a reminder of what a prime number was, he was then able to correctly answer the rest of the questions and reach the Level 4 questions.

Prime Numbers

- One student was stuck on question 4 and kept answering incorrectly. Again, tailored intervention was given before the student became frustrated and he was then able to proceed onto the next level of questions.
- When students were aware that they had given an incorrect answer, they straight away put their hands up to receive support. This then allowed them to progress with increased confidence onto the next questions.

The teacher's evaluation of the lesson

- Using ActivExpression for the activity was great as it really challenged the students. At the end of the activity, they felt confident about applying their knowledge and felt enthused and motivated.
- Some students "panic" in Math so I was able to support them in the Level 1 questions. This gave them the confidence to try the next level of questions and feel as if they had succeeded.
- Students more skilled in Math were determined to reach the Level 5 questions and were engaged throughout the whole activity rather than feeling as if they were waiting for everyone else to catch up.
- The activity also provided me with invaluable feedback.

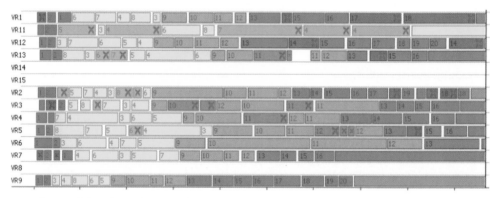

From the results and Excel spreadsheet, it was possible to see that several children fully understood the concept of prime numbers and factors, and so I then moved them onto another activity.

The students' evaluation of the lesson

- Using the handsets is a fun way of doing school work. I really like using the handsets as they are an excellent way to learn and make the lessons much more interesting.
- You can check your answers straightaway, and you can see how well you are doing and then know what you need to improve to get better.
- I like the handsets because the teacher can set levels so that the questions get harder. I believe that we get more attention as the teacher can see straightaway that we are doing well and praise us.

Thanks to Venke Robertshaw from Bournemouth Collegiate School, UK, for this contribution.

*"The guidance on ActivExpression was like I had my
own personal tutor there helping me."*

Student in the class

The challenge

Many learners lack confidence in working through problems without the teacher's
constant attention. In large classes, this presents a problem and ActivExpression can be
used not just for questions but also guidance.

Aims of the lesson

The purpose of the lesson was to monitor the students through multistep algebra
problems. The students would attempt to complete the problems using the Self-Paced
mode. Each step of the task had prompts on the handset to help them.

Target teaching group

This lesson was taught in 5th grade to students with various abilities, but it can be
adjusted to accommodate any age and level.

Context

Prior to the lesson, the multistep problems were introduced to the students, and several
were completed as a whole-class activity. The problems can be basic algebra problems
using PEDMAS or word problems that contain several steps.

How the lesson was organized

Students were given a multistep algebra problem to complete. Several completed the
problem quickly while others struggled. As I walked around the classroom, I noticed that
several were making errors, but the students who were already complete, however, were
ready to move on.

I then started the Self-Paced portion of the lesson, which lasted about 8 minutes. The
students were given another algebra problem and instructed to attempt to solve each
step without assistance, but they were told to check the ActivExpression to see what the
first step was supposed to be. They then entered the answer to the first step on the
ActivExpression and tried to attempt the second step.

Students who had struggled with the layers of steps previously found success with the
assistance of the ActivExpression. Students who had seemed overwhelmed with the
problems loved the fact that they were experiencing success and enjoyed that they were
being guided through the problem. They felt as if they were completing the problem on
their own, and there was a very positive energy in the room.

I monitored the progress on the ActivBoard, and I moved to assist students who were
taking longer to enter their answers. As a final question, I added an entire algebra
equation that the students would have to complete without receiving each step on the
Self-Paced system. This allowed me to meet the needs of the more advanced students
while giving every child in the class an opportunity to finish the first problem.

Using ActivExpression for Guidance

As the more advanced students finished the final problem, every child had completed the first problem and we joined together as a class to review.

How the data from the Self-Paced session was subsequently used

I was able to view the progress chart to see which steps of the problem caused the most trouble. I noticed that the students wanted to multiply before they divided, even when division came first in the problem. This is a common error, because in PEMDAS, the M comes before the D, but you are supposed to perform which operation comes first, be it multiplication or division.

I prepared a homework sheet that only focused on problems of that nature, and I was able to immediately address the error where the students were having difficulty.

The guidance and feedback

During this lesson, the classroom was electric! Every child was enjoying tackling the extremely long and difficult problems, and they liked having the ActivExpression guiding them through the process. For the next day's lesson, I became less specific with the steps provided on the ActivExpression. For example, instead of saying (5 x -2) was the next step, I just had clues, such as:

> *"Don't forget to start in the parenthesis! When you multiply a positive by a negative, your answer is always negative!"*

The lesson was so successful that I started to use the idea with all types of multistep problems. For example:

James needs to buy 10 hotdogs. The hotdogs originally cost $3.00 each. They are currently 20% off. How much would James have to pay?

On the Activexpression, the first step may say:

> *"Remember to figure out how much 1 hotdog would cost with the discount."*

The students would then enter $2.40, and the following comment would appear:

> *"HOT DIGGITY DOG!"*

The next step may say:

> *"Now figure out how much you would have to pay if you purchased 10 at that price."*

That is a simple 2-step problem, but it got the students used to the system, and we were able to progress to problems that had 5–10 steps, and the students were able to handle them with ease.

Feedback from students

During this activity the students were completely focused and intense. They wanted to do well and they were thoroughly driven to finish the task successfully. Quotes collected afterward included:

- I loved to complete the entire problem myself! It was the first one I got correct, but now that I've seen each step and completed it on my own, I know I can do it again.
- That was fun! I was trying to finish before my friends, and I was enjoying it even though it was algebra and I usually don't do well in that subject.
- I felt confident I knew how to do the problem, but the guide let me know I had just made a silly mistake. Having the guide there helped me and pointed out my error. It was like I had my own personal tutor there helping me.
- I was very excited during the lesson. I am a really good math student and I thought I was finished, but then the last problem was a doozy. Mr. Clark put a challenging final problem in the last position, and I liked that because it pushed me to go even further and get it correct.

Other contexts for this idea

Guiding the students through steps can be used with any multistep math problem, but it can also be used for writing an essay. You can guide the students through the thought process for formulating their ideas and preparing their outline. You can also guide them through science experiments or through art activities.

Thanks to Ron Clark, Ron Clark Academy, Atlanta, Georgia, for this contribution.

Personal Relationships

"The ActivExpression handsets are important because if you take a test on one, think about all of the students in every class. You are saving one or two hundred copies every test probably, which is like thousands of pieces of paper every year."

Student in the class

The challenge
It is vitally important that young people learn about personal relationships, reproduction, parenthood, and related health issues such as sexually transmitted infections. Because it is a sensitive subject, it is notoriously difficult to assess exactly what they know, what worries them, and what help or advice they need. ActivExpression can help overcome this problem.

Aims of the lesson
To assess student learning about the anatomy and reproduction health standards after a seven-day presentation from guest speakers.

Target teaching group
This test was administered to four groups of 7th-grade science students (ages 12–13) including an honor's class, an English learner's class, and several students with special needs.

Context
Students have received seven lessons from Planned Parenthood covering dating violence, emotional changes during puberty, anatomy, sexually transmitted infections, and birth control.

The questions
Students use the response devices to take this 18-question Self-Paced test. Some of them are set out at the top of the next page.

The questions include 7 true/false questions, 7 multiple-choice questions with one correct answer, 1 multiple-choice question with more than one correct answer, 1 question that requires a numerical response, and 2 short-answer questions that require a text response. The wide range of question types (i.e. multiple choice with 6 possible choices or 3 correct answers) allows the test to be far more rigorous than typical multiple-choice tests. Questions are read aloud and/or paraphrased for English learners and students with special needs.

	Question	Question Type
1	Text: Explain why women who have unprotected sex should be more concearned with the risk of STIs than the risk of pregnanc...	Text
2	Which 3 fluids contain STIs, but NOT sperm?	Multiple Choice
3	Barrier methods of birth control:	Multiple Choice
4	Which of the following is FALSE about hormonal methods of birth control? They:	Multiple Choice
5	It is normal for some people to be attracted to boys and some people to be attracted to girls (it's OK to be gay, straight, bisexual...	Yes/No
6	Masturbation is extremely dangerous and abnormal.	Yes/No
7	A fertalized egg (zygote) grows into a baby in a woman's:	Multiple Choice
8	Which of the following statements are TRUE about a woman's period?	Multiple Choice
9	Barrier methods prevent ONLY STIs	Yes/No
10	Hormonal methods prevent ONLY pregnancy	Yes/No
11	This change is ABNORMAL during puberty:	Multiple Choice
12	Text in one characteristic of an abusive relationship (physical or emotional) [2 points]	Text
13	Condoms are the most effective method of preventing STIs AND pregnancy in sexually active people.	Yes/No
14	Abstinence:	Multiple Choice

How is the data from the assessment used?

The results of the test are used to guide the instructor's teaching of the health standards based on what the students have learned from the guest speakers. The test results are monitored and saved in ActivInspire (see opposite and below).

The bar graphs below show how students coped with each question and how long they took, and the chart opposite analyzes each student's performance, question by question.

	Level 1		
Name	✓	✗	⏱
1	0	0	0:00
10	9	9	0.27
11	10	8	0.25
12	10	8	0:37
13	12	6	0.45

	Level 1		
Name	✓	✗	⏱
1	0	0	0:00
10	9	9	0.27
11	10	8	0.25
12	10	8	0.37
13	12	6	0.42
14	5	13	0.42
15	13	5	0.51
16	8	10	0.29
17	12	6	0.51
18	12	6	0.43
19	8	10	0.40
2	6	12	0.29
20	6	12	0.38
21	12	6	0.36
22	7	11	0.49
23	0	0	0:00
24	8	10	0.34
25	9	9	0.44
26	6	12	0.21
27	0	0	0:00
28	0	0	0:00
29	0	0	0:00
3	9	9	0.25
30	0	0	0.00
31	0	0	0:00
32	1	0	0:17
4	16	2	0:31
5	13	5	0.44
6	12	6	0:50
7	13	5	0.40
8	8	10	0.59
9	12	6	0.39

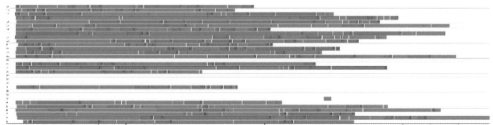

Personal Relationships

The results are then exported to Excel. A snapshot of the diagram is below.

Student Name	1	2	3	5	8	7
Student ID						
Total	18	18	18	18	18	18
%	44%	56%	56%	56%	44%	89%
Total Response Time	728.9	421.4	622.2	867.5	701.5	481.1
Q1	because theyre for life and could cause infections or symptoms	they didnt use protection so they are at a risk for sti's	because the partner may have a diseases	it is more risky to have sti's than to be pregnt becuase you could abort the baby or give it	because they could get a disease like that	because some stis could kill you
Q2	AF	ACDF	ACF	E	AF	ACD
Q3	E	A	E	A	F	A
Q4	F	E	E	D	D	A
Q5	Yes	Yes	Yes	Yes	Yes	Yes
Q6	No	No	No	No	No	No
Q7	A	B	C	D	A	A
Q8	D	C	D	C	C	C
Q9	No	No	No	No	Yes	No
Q10	No	Yes	No	No	Yes	No
Q11	D	D	D	A	B	D
Q12	hitting	screaming	raping and blaming	phyisicel is to hit and emotional is to break up with them	jealous	hitting
Q13	No	No	Yes	No	Yes	Yes
Q14	A	A	D	A	D	A
Q15	Yes	Yes	No	Yes	Yes	Yes
Q16	No	Yes	No	No	Yes	No
Q17	B	B	B	B	A	B
Q18	3	30	12	3	3	10

Students are able to see their test scores at the end of class, and the instructor is able to plan instruction for the remaining lessons on this health standard based on the needs of each class. Without ActivExpression, the teacher would have had to produce this data manually, which would have taken hours of work.

The teacher's evaluation of the lesson
- Would you believe that my students love test day? Since we started using ActivExpression to take our tests, students are more engaged, quiet, and focused.
- They feel like tests are important because they are modeled after the same format that many colleges use to give exams. Furthermore, students are motivated to behave appropriately so that they can view their individual results at the end of class.
- The instant scoring allows me to differentiate instruction for each group the next day, while students immediately know what they need to study in order to improve.

The students' evaluation of the lesson
- I like being able to see my grade at the end of class. When you study really hard, it is a relief to know that you did well on the test!
- Taking tests on the response devices is cool because it is just like texting your teacher. It makes it seem less intimidating than bubbling in answers.

Other contexts for this idea
This test could be given as a pre-assessment. As a result of the "export to Excel" feature, color-coding, and percentage correct analysis features, student pre-tests and post-assessments can easily be compared to evaluate growth in student learning in every content standard.

Thanks to Kat Czujko, Hollenbeck Middle School, Los Angles, California, for this contribution.

*"The students love using ActivExpression.
I can assess them without them even realizing that
I am doing so!"*

Teacher in the Fraction Quest lesson

The challenge

Many learners grow up phobic about Math, particularly if they find it difficult. Teachers sometimes find ingenious ways to remove the fear and improve skills while making it fun.

Aims of the lesson

All learners were required to:

- follow oral and written directions; divide words into fractional parts;
- use equivalent fractions to correctly divide words; decode words.

Target teaching group

The activity is used with students in Grade 3. The students' Math ability levels range from basic to advanced.

Context

A unit on fractions has been presented to students. Students have had practice identifying and naming fractions of a unit and fractions of a group. They have learned how to write fractions. Equivalent fractions for ½ and ¼ have been introduced. Students perform word-building activities during language arts instruction on a regular basis. Students have used ActivExpression frequently and are proficient at toggling back and forth between lowercase, uppercase, and numbers.

Important

In this lesson, all students had their own computer—the Self-Paced questions were on the teacher's computer but the students were able to move through the flipchart on their own screens.

How the lesson began

The activity was introduced by discussing what the detective on Page 1 of the flipchart was doing. What is a quest? The teacher explained that they would be going on a quest for a mystery object and that the students' knowledge of fractions and word-building skills would be used to solve the mystery.

The teacher then reminded them of what makes a fraction and asked them to switch on their ActivExpression handsets. The teacher asked them to click on the "Directions" button on the flipchart, which brought up a pdf of the instructions. They were told to complete the Level 1 and Level 2 questions on their ActivExpression handsets.

	Question	Question Type	Level
1	The top number in a fraction tells how many equal parts are being used. It is called the:	Multiple Choice	Level 1
2	3/4 is a fraction. 4 is the:	Multiple Choice	Level 1
3	Are you ready to go on a FRACTION QUEST?	Yes/No	Level 2
4	Use the flipchart pages to build the correct words. Make sure you pay attention to capitalization and punctuation. DO NOT SEND YO...	Text	Level 3

They were reminded **not** to send in answers for the Level 3 question until the end of the flipchart!

How the lesson progressed

Level 3 Question: Students had to build words by dividing words into fractional parts. They had to solve the mystery message: **Knowing your fractions can earn you 100 Grand. There can be no mistakes!** The students were told to move onto their own computers and work through the flipcharts, texting in on ActivExpression the words that they solved, but not clicking "send" until the end. Each screen held fraction/word clues like the one below.

Using their knowledge of fractions, each student dragged out the letters (see image on the right above) from the bottom of the flipchart to form the right word. Similar clues followed on the next pages. The teacher intervened a number of times including when one student misread the "last ¼" instead of "first ¼." She froze the activity and asked him to explain what he had done—she described this as an "awesome teachable moment" which had a great impact because a student was able to reinforce the need to follow directions carefully. Once the final sentence had been solved, they had to use ActivExpression to text in their sentences. Those who got the sentence and punctuation right won 100 Grand awards!

Knowing your fractions can earn you 100 Grand. There can be no mistakes!

How the feedback from the Self-Paced session was used

The feedback enabled the teacher to assess each of the four skills identified in the lesson aims and then plan future support for individuals who had areas of strength or weakness.

The teacher's evaluation of the lesson

- This lesson provided authentic assessment. The students did a fantastic job of texting and enjoyed sharing their answers in this manner.
- Students loved building the words on the flipchart. The hands-on component kept them motivated.
- You could have "heard a pin drop" in the room during this activity and that does not happen very often.
- Math, language arts, and technology were integrated into one lesson and the students were learning and having fun by actively participating in the lesson.

The students' evaluation of the lesson

- "Can we do this again tomorrow" – One male student with behavior issues who was the first one to successfully complete the fraction activity and receive the 100 Grand award.

A few students did not finish the activity BUT did not want to stop to go to lunch:

- "These fractions are cool!"
- "I didn't know you could divide words into fractions."
- "We don't want to go to lunch, can we finish first?"—A small group who were having so much fun they wanted to delay eating!
- "I could picture the fractions as I was making the words."—One student who usually struggles in Math.

Thanks to Barb Knapp, Meadowbrook Elementary School, Rapid City, South Dakota, for this contribution.

Beat my Best

"ActivExpression is highly effective for this type of activity, randomizing the questions and analyzing the results instantly; they don't have to wait for the marking!"

The teacher for this lesson

The challenge
Regular testing can be boring and cause anxiety. In this lesson, they look forward to tests.

Aims of the lesson
The teacher assesses the progress of all the students in basic Math skills with a "Beat my best" activity, where students try to beat their previous best score.

Target teaching group
9- and 10-year olds.

Context
The idea is to give tests at regular intervals, encouraging the students to master these skills in a fun way.

How does the lesson work?
The teacher prepares a Self-Paced set of over 70 questions in mental Math. In the examples below, they are all adding or multiplying questions, although the same idea would work with other types of calculation. Some of the questions are shown below.

	Question	Question Type	Level	Options	Correct Answers
1	5+2	Numeric	Level 1		7
2	9x9	Numeric	Level 1		81
3	6+4	Numeric	Level 1		10
4	9+4	Numeric	Level 1		13
5	6+5	Numeric	Level 1		11
6	7x3	Numeric	Level 1		21
7	9+7	Numeric	Level 1		16
8	5+4	Numeric	Level 1		9
9	9+8	Numeric	Level 1		17
10	8x7	Numeric	Level 1		56

The Response Revolution

The teacher has set the questions to randomize and it means that the questions, all at Level 1, will appear on handsets in a random order; no one will get the same questions in sequence so students won't be able to copy friends.

How the lesson progressed
The students know that they have 3 minutes to answer as many questions as possible. No intervention is allowed. A musical countdown starts and then the teacher starts the Self-Paced. When the 3 minutes is up, a musical "gong" ends the test. Scores are revealed. Students compare their scores from the previous week and improvements are celebrated.

The teacher's evaluation of the lesson
- I am able to use the feedback to identify class issues and those that only relate to small groups or individuals. This information helps future lesson planning.
- The students are highly motivated by this weekly test and they are all determined to beat their previous best. It is not an issue if their score is lower than a friend's as long as they improve.

The students' evaluation of the lesson
- I found I was typing more quickly than writing so it saved time—it wasn't like doing a test!
- You had to concentrate to make sure you pressed the right button—this helped me focus more with fewer distractions.
- I really like comparing the scores from week to week.

Thanks to Anthony Smith, Sunderland High Junior School, Sunderland, UK, for this contribution.

"No amount of energy will take the place of thought. A strenuous life with its eyes shut is a kind of wild insanity."

Henry Van Dyke

The challenge

Many young people and adults form opinions on first impressions or prejudices and are unable to see alternative viewpoints.

Aims of the lesson

The purpose of this lesson is to develop the thinking skills of the students using Edward de Bono's "six hats" technique. This technique will work in most areas of the curriculum and with most ages. It encourages learners to look at the same issue from a range of different perspectives. It is also excellent for developing students' skills in speaking and debating.

Target teaching group

Any age.

Context

The class has been organized into small groups, each of which has one ActivExpression handset registered as Group 1, Group 2, and so on. The flipchart on the interactive whiteboard below identifies the issue for debate—Should countries use Nuclear Power?

De Bono's six hats

There are 6 colored hats in de Bono's thinking skills technique. These are color-coded on the spinning wheel on the flipchart. Each of the hats represents a different type of thinking.

White	Facts. Objective views. No bias. What do we know? What do we need to know? How do we find out?
Red	Emotions. What do we like or dislike? How do we feel?
Black	Critical. Will it work? What are the dangers or problems? What questions?
Yellow	Positive. Why is it a good idea? How will it work?
Green	New thinking. What else can we do? How can it be modified? New approach?
Blue	Planning. The thinking process. Setting up the procedures and rules.

How the lesson works

1. The lesson aims and the features of the different hats are explained and all groups now wear the blue hat for five minutes to discuss the rules they think should be followed. Self-Paced question 1 now asks them to text in 2 suggested rules.

2. The rules are seeded to a blank screen and after a short discussion the rules are agreed.

3. The teacher spins the wheel on the flipchart and colored hats are allocated to each group. Ten minutes are allocated for discussion on Nuclear Power, with each group keeping to the philosophy of the color they represent. Self-Paced question 2 asks each group to text in 3 points the group has agreed on. These are seeded to the flipchart below.

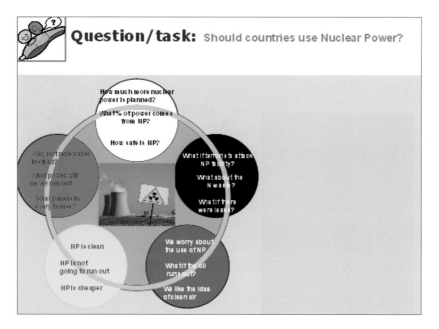

Question/task: Should countries use Nuclear Power?

The Self-Paced function allows the groups to send one issue at a time. At the end of the process, the results browser is opened and each of the 3 responses from each group are seeded to the screen and grouped in the panel on the right. Text colors can be changed if necessary and then the points are dragged into the appropriate circle.

The debate can now begin with each group justifying its points. The method used here to reach the debate has a number of benefits:

1. Using ActivExpression allows seeding of ideas which will produce a final image (as above) which can be printed as a poster or handout if further work is planned.
2. The groups need to collaborate in addressing the issues and then agreeing their key points.
3. The allocation of a color forces students to think more widely and consider viewpoints they may not have previously considered.

Alternative approach

The first stage, where all the groups wear the blue hat, is repeated. From then on, however, each group can receive a series of Self-Paced messages such as:

- Now send a yellow key point
- Now send a green point
- Now send a white key point

and so on. In this way, each group will have to consider each viewpoint before the debate.

Grateful thanks to the United Church Schools Trust in the UK for permission to adapt some flipchart pages from their forthcoming training materials "ActivExpression for Learning."

"It amazes me that when I hand a rowdy set of 7th-graders an ActivExpression and they press the 'go' button, heads go down, focusing on the questions and answers they are going to input. I think I actually see smoke from hard-working brains."

The teacher of this lesson

The challenge

Many teachers face classes with occasional rowdy behavior. Motivating them to stay on task is a big challenge, particularly in Math if some of them see it as a "weak" subject. This teacher uses ActivExpression in an interesting "station" or "circus" arrangement with four separate activities in the classroom, one of which makes use of ActivExpression.

Aims of the lesson

The aim of this lesson was for students to use a non-traditional method of review for the State test. The topic was Pre-Algebra.

Target teaching group

This is for a group of 7th-graders (ages 12–14) with varied ability ranges in Pre-Algebra.

Context

Students have been working for all the school year on 13 different but connected Pre-Algebra units. The teacher has prepared Self-Paced review questions to be used in a "scavenger hunt" style of activity where the questions on the Self-Paced screen direct them to an existing course book to find the answers. This was one of the first times that the teacher had used ActivExpression with this class.

The questions

The questions are differentiated from Level 1 to Level 7 and include responses of all kinds: multiple choice, text, numeric, and Likert scale.

Fractions from Textbook Activity

	Question	Question Type	Level
1	On page 227, What is the answer to number 7?	Multiple Choice	Level 1
2	How well do you know the other properties of integers?	Likert Scale	Level 1
3	On page 237, number 12, what if there were no peanuts added, how much would the ingre…	Text	Level 1
4	Go back to page 229, What is the answer to number 25?	Multiple Choice	Level 2
5	What operation would you use on number 18 of page 239?	Text	Level 2
6	How do you feel about the geometry on page 247?	Likert Scale	Level 3
7	So try number 3 on page 247 - don't forget inches over feet in both fractions.	Multiple Choice	Level 3
8	You're almost finished, on pg. 242 figure out the answer for number 2.	Multiple Choice	Level 5
9	Now what is the final price?	Multiple Choice	Level 5
10	If the answer was in the form of PI, what page would that be?	Numeric	Level 5
11	Which page has a positive correlation scatterplot?	Numeric	Level 5
12	On pg. 243, What operation do you do with the exponents for number 13?	Text	Level 6
13	So the answer would be???	Multiple Choice	Level 6
14	What page has a cubic slope pictured?	Numeric	Level 6
15	the surface area question on pg 261 is related to what question on what page?	Multiple Choice	Level 7

How the lesson progressed

The teacher organized four "station" activities. One was making use of ActivExpression and there were three other stations going on at the same time. Each group would spend an allocated time at each of the stations during the lesson. She had baskets of ActivExpressions, and whiteboards with markers available. One student, who was in charge of the station, started the session by pressing the green, Self-Paced button and the students used their books and whiteboards to answer questions on the ActivExpressions. One student printed the results at the end of the station.

The teacher also asked the students to record their answers in a journal, which were used as notes for homework. Two groups had to be redirected during their Self-Paced station time. The teacher felt that there might have been too many questions to keep it interesting for some of the students. She thought the lesson worked well because she was able to watch her students go through the book and read the questions on ActivExpression, knowing that they were not just copying from a friend.

Fractions from Textbook Activity

How the feedback was used

The four-station approach meant that the teacher was unable to make use of the live feedback provided by ActivExpression during the lesson. Because she was new to the technology, she was pleased with the data that was produced by each of the groups on the ActivExpression station and realized how useful it might be in the future:

- It identified which students had mastered particular areas of Pre-Algebra.
- It showed how some topics needed more whole-class revision.
- It helped individual students to target topics they needed to revise for the tests.

The teacher's evaluation of the lesson

- This was a very satisfying lesson—the kids loved so much to work in small group stations.
- Watching the students interact with the technology and being engaged in their own learning was powerful. It was amazing to have technology in my room that students would actually enjoy using and not act like they had done this a million times.
- This was my first year with 7th-graders and I was nervous that they would not react as well as my 6th-graders. ActivExpression brought a new excitement—they look and act like cell phones—and the kids reacted to and interacted in Math of all things.
- Watching their faces as they got the questions wrong (or right) and what they did next to go on with their lesson was priceless. When their time was up for their station, they didn't want to leave.
- I could tell that at least they were excited about doing a review in this type of situation, that there was some form of learning going on. They also like watching the screen to see how everyone else is doing with their questions.

The students' evaluation of the lesson

- I liked it when I got a message on my handset that said "ehhhh, try again" when I got one answer wrong.
- When I got an answer right, the message on the handset said "U R a math Wiz." I liked that!
- I liked not having to wait for others in the class who are slower than me.
- We like this way of working. It's how we talk to our friends—by texting.

Thanks to Susan Lehr, C. Todd Clark Intermediate School, Clovis Unified, California, for this contribution.

US Football

"The students truly loved this game! The room-sized football field enabled the students to be moving throughout the lesson, and my kinesthetic learners were incredibly engaged."

The teacher of this class

The challenge

Handled sensitively, competitive games can be a great motivator. Many students, boys and girls, are sports mad and this ingenious lesson uses a US national sport to engage students in what is usually a dry subject—English grammar!

Aims of the lesson

Students were required to identify independent and subordinate clauses as well as simple, compound, complex, and compound-complex sentences.

Target teaching group

This specific lesson could be used with language arts students in grades 5–9 (ages 10–15), depending on the complexity of the sentences given.

Context

Several strategies had already been used to teach the students how to identify clauses and sentence types, including concept attainment, New American Lecture, and cooperative group games. The students were also taught a song about types of sentences.

The questions

There were 20 Self-Paced instructions or questions in the set—most of them are shown below. They range from Level 1 to Level 5.

	Question	Question Type	Level	Options
1	A simple sentence has	Multiple Choice	Level 1	1 ind. clause; 2 ii
2	A compound sentence has	Multiple Choice	Level 1	1 ind clause; 2 su
3	The players were talented, and they worked well together.	Multiple Choice	Level 2	S; C; CX; C-CX
4	Although she is often grumpy, I still enjoy her company.	Multiple Choice	Level 2	S; C; CX; C-CX
5	The little girl in the red sweater is the fastest runner on the team.	Multiple Choice	Level 2	S; C; CX; C-CX
6	I love to watch them play on the field; they seem to enjoy themselves.	Multiple Choice	Level 3	S; C; CX; C-CX
7	If you will help me with the groceries, I will make you dinner.	Multiple Choice	Level 3	S; C; CX; C-CX
8	Since she started school, she has been studying every night.	Multiple Choice	Level 3	S; C; CX; C-CX
9	The dinner was excellent, and I was too full to eat dessert.	Multiple Choice	Level 4	S; C; CX; C-CX
10	We need to thank him whenever he offers his help.	Multiple Choice	Level 4	S; C; CX; C-CX
11	The little girl in the red sweater is the fastest runner on the team.	Multiple Choice	Level 4	S; C; CX; C-CX
12	I will watch the movie as soon as I finish reading my book.	Multiple Choice	Level 5	S; C; CX; C-CX
13	The children whom I teach are brilliant.	Multiple Choice	Level 5	S; C; CX; C-CX

All the questions were multiple choice and involved very careful reading of the sentences sent to the handsets. Two examples of the questions are below.

Adjective clauses begin with:
A. a subordinating conjunction
B. a coordinating conjunction
C. a relative pronoun
D. an adjective

I ran in the marathon and I was so proud of myself.
A. simple
B. compound
C. complex
D. compound-complex

How the lesson was organized

Prior to the lesson: The teacher cleared all desks and chairs from the center of the classroom. Using masking tape, she created football-field yard lines by taping evenly spaced parallel lines on the floor.

During the lesson: Students were divided into 2 football teams, the red team and the blue team. (The teacher obtained colored pinnies from the PE department, and the students wore these throughout the lesson.) Each student was given an ActivExpression and a die.

The two teams started behind the end zones at the opposite ends of the field. Self-Paced questions about clauses and types of sentences were given. Each time the student answered a question correctly, the ActivExpression told them to "Roll for yardage." The student rolled his/her die, and then he/she advanced the number of yard lines that were rolled. If a student answered incorrectly, the ActivExpression said "Fumble!" and no yardage was gained. Lively football music played throughout the room during the lesson.

Whenever a student crossed the end zone, he/she raised their hands in the air to denote a touchdown. The teacher recorded this, and the player started to advance in the other direction on the football field. At the end of the lesson, the team with the most overall touchdowns won.

Throughout the lesson, the teacher walked through the class, monitoring progress and helping students. In addition to seeing the progress on the screen, it was easy for the teacher to get a visual of the students' progress by watching when the students rolled the dice and when they were stationary.

How the data from the Self-Paced session was subsequently used

Student data was used to determine which students needed more practice and which needed to be challenged with even more difficult examples. This information was also used during students' writing conferences to ensure that students' essays included the varied types of sentences we were studying.

The teacher's evaluation of the lesson

- The students truly loved this game! The room-sized football field enabled the students to be moving throughout the lesson, and my kinesthetic learners were incredibly engaged. The game couldn't operate without the Self-Paced function offered by ActivExpression.
- Students were extremely careful when answering questions because they knew that they could only advance yardage if they were correct the first time that they responded.
- By allowing students to receive touchdowns throughout the game, the students received encouragement throughout the task, not just at the end.
- Finally, the students loved the idea that there was a little luck involved, too. A lucky roll of the die could give a child a jump start, and this made all learners feel like they had a shot at contributing to the team score.
- Just four days after implementing this lesson, my class asked if we could do it again with different content.

The students' evaluation of the lesson

- That was as exciting as playing in a real football game!
- I was being so careful because I wanted to help my team score.
- I love the instant feedback with the Self-Paced tests.
- It is impossible ever to be bored with these!

Other contexts for this activity

This game could easily be altered to be played as soccer or baseball. Using the same concept, the students would advance down the field or around the bases as correct answers were given.

In soccer, the two teams might compete for possession by answering questions correctly, with the results being shown after an agreed number of questions. The team with the best score has a chance at scoring a goal. The goal-scoring question is sent to the handsets and if the shooting team gets the most right answers, they score a goal, but if the defending team does best then they save it and have possession for the next round of questions.

The basic premise of this game could be used with any Self-Paced questions, regardless of the academic concept being reviewed. So it would work in any subject, with any age, and with any size of class, provided that the classroom is big enough.

With a laptop, this would also work outside if a space can be laid with the appropriate markings.

Thanks to Kim Bearden, Ron Clark Academy, Atlanta, Georgia, for this contribution.

Publishing Partners

Promethean has established commercial partnerships with a number of companies that develop educational programs that are compatible with ActivExpression. Two companies and three programs are featured in this section: Robert Powell Publications Ltd with EyeWrite and Race Game, and Learning Clip with its online Math program.

EyeWrite visual planning software

"Many young people find it difficult to plan writing or speaking; the task of organizing and structuring paragraphs and sections is a real problem. This software, compatible with ActivExpression, is designed to help this process."

Robert Powell

Why is EyeWrite different?

Most visual planning programs start with a blank screen, and words and images are added to form a "map."

This is not the way teachers would do it. Most teachers helping learners to plan a project will encourage learners to begin by compiling a list of ideas or topics for the work. After all, you can't start *organizing* the project until you have all the ideas together. That is how EyeWrite works; collect the ideas first, then map them. The example that follows shows the process for planning a project on "Saving animals."

EyeWrite

The finished product

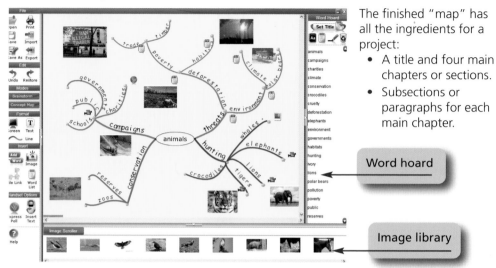

The finished "map" has all the ingredients for a project:

- A title and four main chapters or sections.
- Subsections or paragraphs for each main chapter.

Word hoard

Image library

How was this visual plan produced?

Stage 1. Compile the list of ideas.

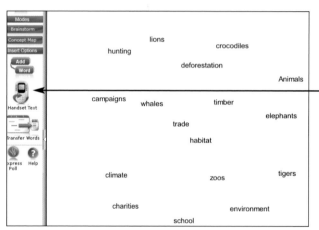

Commentary

The teacher says:
"Text a mammal"
and clicks on the ActivExpression icon. Learners text and words appear on the screen.
"Now text a 'threat'."
The process is repeated. More words appear.
"Now text a type of campaign to save animals."
*The process is repeated—more words appear. The ideas grow with contributions from **all** students.*

Stage 2. Click "**Transfer words**"— they go to the "Word hoard."

Stage 3. Right-click in the image library and import images from a previously prepared folder of animal images.

Stage 4. Select title (Animals), click on "Set Title" at top of Word Hoard, and the title appears in the middle. Discuss main headings with class and ask students to drag out words to link with heading.

Now teachers have the main headings, there are two choices:

1. Allow students individually to choose the subheadings or paragraphs by selecting from the work hoard.

2. Design a class map with all students' contributing ideas.

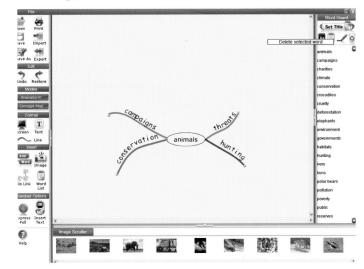

Stage 5. Change color of background and/or lines using toolbars.

Stage 6. Click on "**File Link**" and add a photograph, video clip, flash file, website, or sound clip to any word that you select. Icons appear to show the link. Double-click on an icon and the link opens. These links allow the visual plan to be used as a stimulus.

Stage 7. Add text. Right-click on any word and select "Show notes" and either the teacher or the students can add text. If the students are working on their own computers, all the writing for the project can be done in this way.

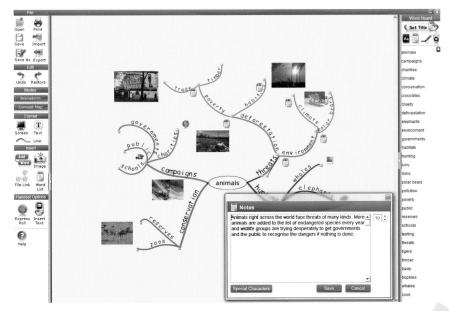

EyeWrite

A notes icon appears next to the word where writing has been added—you will see that on the visual plan above, the "Threats" section has been finished because it has a notes icon against each key word.

Stage 8. Turn the visual plan into a Word document.

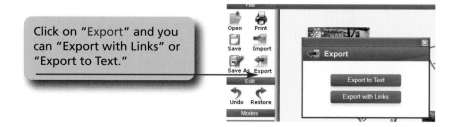

> Click on "Export" and you can "Export with Links" or "Export to Text."

1. "Export with Links" allows you to export the whole visual plan, with all the hyperlinks intact, to a folder of your choice so that others can use it. This helps where teachers in a school or even a District want to share the production of visual plans and use each other's.

2. "Export to Text" allows you to save the text that you have added and then open it in Word. See the text below—it matches the organization of the visual map. The "branches" have become paragraphs.

animals

threats
Animals right across the world face threats of many kinds. More animals are added to the list of endangered species every year and wildlife groups are trying desperately to get governments and the public to recognise the dangers if nothing is done.

environment
Changes to the environment are one of the major concerns for wildlife experts. Global warming is predicted to have a huge imapct upon both human and animal life with some parts of the world due to be under water within 100 years.

climate
Changes to the climate are having an impact upon wildlife in many parts of the world. The thickness of the ice in the polar caps is reported to be getting thinner and thinner every decade and this will almost certainly result in the extiction of animals such as Polar Bears that depend upon the ice.

polar bears
Polar Bears depend upon the ice to hunt for seal. If the ice disappears then they will find it almost impossible to eat because in the water seals swim much faster than Polar Bears and will get away very easily if attacked.

deforestation
One of the major problems facing animals is the loss of habitat and in some

The essay or project is not finished, but it is now in a draft form with a well-organized paragraph structure. It will delight learners who are often anxious when they see a blank page and know they have to fill it with writing! They can now improve it by adding connectives, but the key purpose of a well-planned piece of writing has been achieved.

EyeWrite is only in PC format at present, but the cost of a site license is less than a quarter of other visual mapping programs and with its link to ActivExpression and its drag-and-drop functions, it is very much the best program for class participation.

More information at www.robertpowellpublications.com

Using ActivExpression with Learning Clip

Learning Clip is the first commercially developed, online suite of resources for ActivExpression, spanning the full elementary/primary school Math curriculum. The **www.learningclip.com** website offers hundreds of interactive activities, video clips, and worksheets covering a huge range of Math topics, concepts, and methods for students aged 4 to 12.

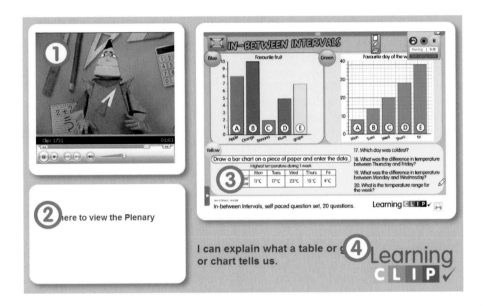

1. Video featuring one of the three Math heroes, *Triangle Man*.
2. Two video parts—introduction and plenary.
3. The interactive activity optimized for use on an interactive whiteboard.
4. The learning objective written clearly beneath each activity.

Learning Clip

These superb videos have two other heroes which younger students love:

Bread Head

Zero Gravity

The resources have been specifically purposed for whole-class teaching with an interactive whiteboard and only use drag-and-drop or point-and-click interaction.

The learner response components are seamlessly integrated into their core interactive whiteboard resources; with a single click the teacher can switch instantly from teaching the whole class with the whiteboard to questioning the class via ActivExpression.

Once in learner response mode, the students can interact with the resources by using ActivExpression. Instead of the question being answered by the teacher clicking a button on the board, the students send their answers via ActivExpression. Once every student has responded, the whole class's performance is displayed on the whiteboard.

Individual and class results can be automatically stored online as a by-product of the teaching. Results can also be exported to Excel.

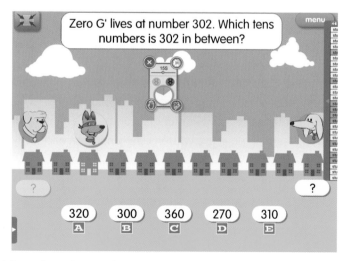

A class list also indicates which students have submitted a response and which have yet to answer. The ActivExpression display is automatically configured to accept appropriate responses relating to each question.

The teacher can position a simple toolbar to start and stop or set a time limit for each question.

A "Dynamic Pie Chart" immediately displays the proportion of correct responses as they are received. The teacher can also call up a detailed breakdown of all the responses so far.

The detailed results are built into a table, with each row representing one student's answers, just like in Inspire. The names can be switched off.

Learning Clip's Math resources can be tried by teachers even if they haven't yet invested in ActivExpression. Visit **www.learningclip.com/free** and you will be able to simulate the ActivExpression experience with a number of free lessons.

The benefit of recording and marking student answers in real time doesn't end when the lesson does. All the answers generated in class can be automatically stored in the teacher's account. This builds into a complete picture of a class's activity and individual student's performance. A comprehensive set of reports provides excellent evidence of pupil progress and support for summative assessments.

Learning Clip

Learning Clip allows teachers to analyze data in a number of ways. For example—a student summary by topic:

Voting Sessions Overview	Student Result List

Student Name	Using & Applying Maths			Understanding Numbers			Number Facts			Calculating			Understanding Shape			Measuring			Handling Data			summary		
	S	A	%	S	A	%	S	A	%	S	A	%	S	A	%	S	A	%	S	A	%	S	A	%
Amy	11	125	39.2	27	354	50.8	17	193	47.2	19	204	47.5	11	147	46.9	17	229	51.5	7	130	53.1	109	1382	48.0
Dominic	11	125	75.2	27	354	77.7	17	193	86.0	19	204	89.2	11	147	78.2	17	229	79.9	7	130	86.2	109	1382	81.8
Edward	11	125	95.2	27	354	89.0	17	193	91.7	19	204	88.7	11	147	71.4	17	229	86.0	7	130	84.6	109	1382	86.7
George	11	125	83.2	27	354	81.4	17	193	74.6	19	204	78.4	11	147	70.7	17	229	80.3	7	130	71.5	109	1382	77.2
Haley	11	125	74.4	27	354	57.3	17	193	59.6	19	204	60.8	11	147	66.0	17	229	68.1	7	130	65.4	109	1382	64.5
Ian	11	125	63.2	27	354	54.5	17	193	64.2	19	204	63.7	11	147	56.5	17	229	55.5	7	130	68.5	109	1382	60.9
Jack	11	125	84.8	27	354	83.6	17	193	78.2	19	204	84.8	11	147	82.3	17	229	79.9	7	130	80.0	109	1382	82.0
James	11	125	84.8	27	354	74.3	17	193	74.6	19	204	77.9	11	147	77.6	17	229	81.2	7	130	73.1	109	1382	77.6
Jane	11	125	74.4	27	354	68.1	17	193	69.9	19	204	70.6	11	147	70.7	17	229	76.0	7	130	66.2	109	1382	70.8
Jennifer	11	125	63.2	27	354	55.6	17	193	59.1	19	204	65.2	11	147	63.9	17	229	59.4	7	130	63.8	109	1382	61.5
Joshua	11	125	70.4	27	354	70.9	17	193	72.5	19	204	73.5	11	147	59.9	17	229	73.8	7	130	80.8	109	1382	71.7
Kyle	11	125	54.4	27	354	53.1	17	193	54.4	19	204	50.5	11	147	51.7	17	229	59.4	7	130	53.8	109	1382	53.9
Lauren	11	125	80.8	27	354	79.9	17	193	83.4	19	204	77.0	11	147	78.9	17	229	80.3	7	130	77.7	109	1382	79.7
Linda	11	125	56.0	27	354	57.3	17	193	61.7	19	204	59.3	11	147	61.9	17	229	54.1	7	130	62.3	109	1382	59.0
Lucy	11	125	56.0	27	354	72.0	17	193	71.5	19	204	69.6	11	147	61.9	17	229	74.7	7	130	64.6	109	1382	67.2
Luke	11	125	89.6	27	354	79.7	17	193	87.6	19	204	86.8	11	147	93.9	17	229	94.3	7	130	88.5	109	1382	88.6
Marcus	11	125	84.8	27	354	87.9	17	193	87.6	19	204	87.3	11	147	97.3	17	229	95.6	7	130	96.9	109	1382	91.0
Martin	11	125	64.0	27	354	66.9	17	193	65.8	19	204	69.1	11	147	69.4	17	229	75.1	7	130	57.7	109	1382	66.9
Mathew	11	125	69.6	27	354	79.4	17	193	86.5	19	204	87.7	11	147	82.3	17	229	80.3	7	130	83.1	109	1382	81.3
Melanie	11	125	41.6	27	354	42.7	17	193	40.9	19	204	48.5	11	147	44.2	17	229	50.2	7	130	54.6	109	1382	46.1
Miles	11	125	68.8	27	354	71.5	17	193	71.0	19	204	71.6	11	147	71.4	17	229	76.0	7	130	46.9	109	1382	68.2
Peter	11	125	83.2	27	354	73.2	17	193	81.9	19	204	81.9	11	147	80.3	17	229	72.9	7	130	83.8	109	1382	79.6
Sally	11	125	55.2	27	354	55.9	17	193	59.6	19	204	54.9	11	147	65.3	17	229	59.4	7	130	52.3	109	1382	57.5
Sam	11	125	64.0	27	354	60.2	17	193	63.7	19	204	59.8	11	147	51.0	17	229	56.8	7	130	70.0	109	1382	60.8
Siobhan	11	125	78.4	27	354	68.9	17	193	72.5	19	204	72.5	11	147	73.5	17	229	75.1	7	130	84.6	109	1382	75.1
Stephen	11	125	69.6	27	354	59.9	17	193	62.7	19	204	65.2	11	147	62.6	17	229	64.2	7	130	40.8	109	1382	60.7
Tariq	11	125	78.4	27	354	79.4	17	193	73.1	19	204	79.9	11	147	72.1	17	229	65.5	7	130	73.8	109	1382	74.6
Toby	11	125	66.4	27	354	64.7	17	193	64.8	19	204	56.9	11	147	63.9	17	229	73.8	7	130	84.6	109	1382	67.9
Tyrone	11	125	87.2	27	354	83.9	17	193	82.4	19	204	86.3	11	147	81.6	17	229	83.8	7	130	71.5	109	1382	82.4
Victoria	11	125	38.4	27	354	45.5	17	193	49.7	19	204	50.0	11	147	45.6	17	229	45.4	7	130	56.2	109	1382	47.3

It also offers:

- Class overview over a specified time
- Class summary by topic
- Class summary by strand (theme)
- Class summary by activity
- Individual student performance by topic, strand, or activity

Following the launch of Learning Clip + Learner Response, the company has begun work on a second phase of development for ActivExpression, this time making use of the asynchronous interaction that the handsets support. Once realized, the new features will allow students to answer questions related to the core Learning Clip resources independently and at their own pace. Work on this system is ongoing, but the early samples show great promise.

For more information visit www.learningclip.com.

Using ActivExpression with the Race Game AfL

"I have never seen a single piece of software that engaged students more than the Race Game. I used it in several third-grade classes and, without fail, EVERY single student was completely engaged in the lesson EVERY time. Not once did I see a student off task."

Sandi H. Dennis, Media and Instructional Technology Specialist,
The 4/5 Academy at Fifth Avenue, Decatur, Georgia

The Race Game on PC or Mac has been developed for use with ActivExpression or ActiVote handsets and can be played individually, or in teams or groups.

How many can play?

Up to 32 cars race around a motor-racing circuit. Each student or team is in a car and they go faster if students get their answers right, and slower if they get them wrong. The excitement in classes is incredible.

Race Game

What kinds of questions?

Multiple-choice. There are databases of over 40,000 questions ready to use for Math, Science and English, from Grade 2 to 12 (7–16 years) but the Race Editor allows you to create your own for any age, difficulty level, or subject. The Math database is coded against State Standards.

Are the questions all text?

No. The software allows questions to be text, images, or sounds so you can involve even those whose reading skills are weak.

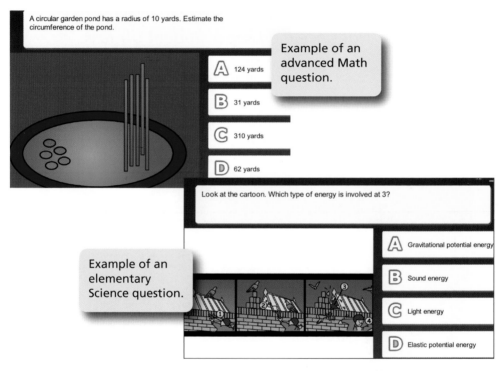

The software records all students' responses, and the reports that are exportable to Excel include:

- An analysis of each individual's performance, question by question
- An analysis of each question and the percentage of students who got it right

The Race Game is ideal for many situations

- End-of-lesson assessment to check on understanding
- Start-of-lesson activity to recap on the previous lesson
- Team collaboration activity to consolidate skills
- Quiz nights with parents

More information at www.robertpowellpublications.com

Assigning student to devices

Teachers can register ActivExpression manually, but to save time it is possible to "assign" handsets to existing class lists.

You can access this function from two locations within ActivInspire.

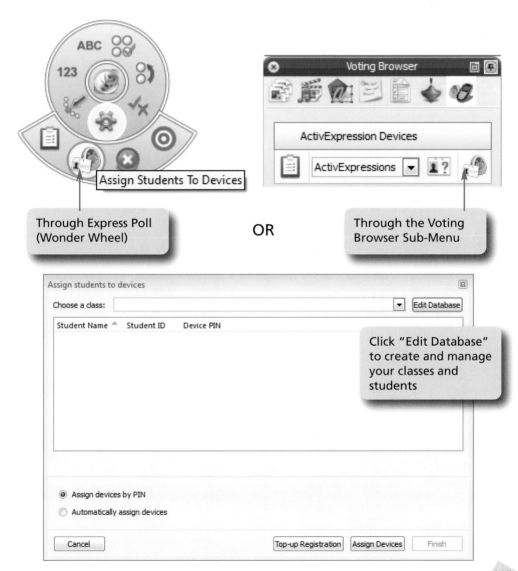

Assigning Students to Devices

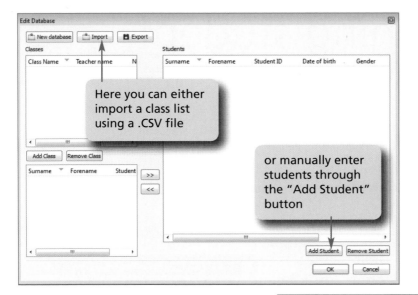

Here you can either import a class list using a .CSV file

or manually enter students through the "Add Student" button

The best way to create your .CSV (comma delimited) file is to use your School Information Management System. Here is a simple list using Microsoft Excel, which can be saved as a .CSV file.

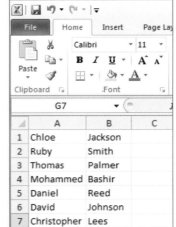

When you come to save you will see the .CSV selection.

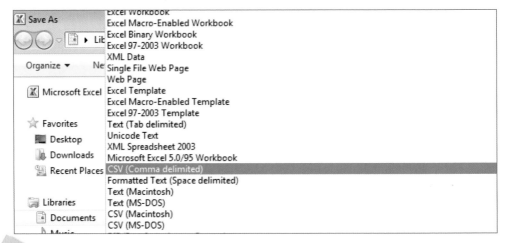

Assigning Students to Devices

After clicking import and selecting your .CSV file, you will then be presented with the following.

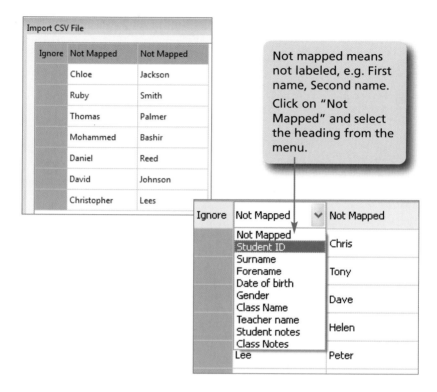

Not mapped means not labeled, e.g. First name, Second name.

Click on "Not Mapped" and select the heading from the menu.

You have now successfully imported your list of students.

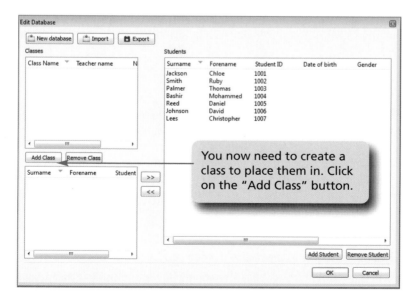

You now need to create a class to place them in. Click on the "Add Class" button.

Assigning Students to Devices

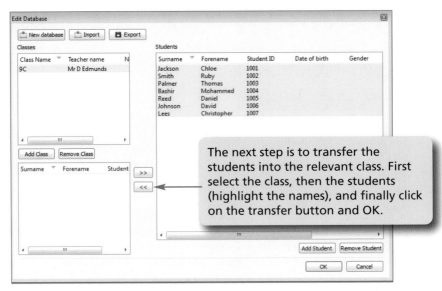

At this point it is advisable to use the "Export" feature to create a backup of your database.

You are now ready to assign your students to handsets.

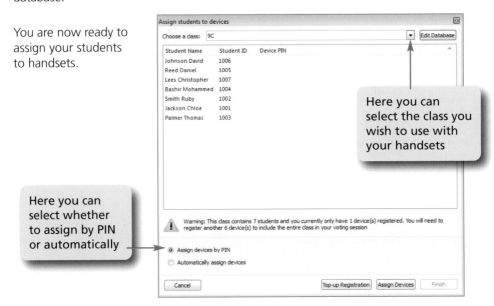

There are two ways now to assign the student names to the handsets. If you select "by PIN" then a three-digit number will be generated next to each student and the student will have to enter this into the handset. The second "Automatically assign" option instantly adds the names of the students to the handsets. Although this option is a simple way to name the handsets, it can be an issue with regard to distribution for larger class sizes.

Once you have been through this process with each class, you will be able to import each class immediately for registration.

Seeding results from the browser

Teachers can use Self-Paced to send a series of ideas, e.g. in text form, and then seed them to the screen. (See *Of Mice and Men* in the Ending Lessons section for an example of this.)

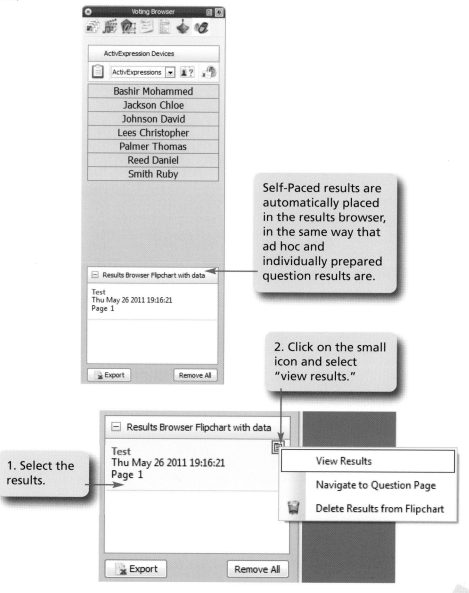

Self-Paced results are automatically placed in the results browser, in the same way that ad hoc and individually prepared question results are.

2. Click on the small icon and select "view results."

1. Select the results.

Seeding Results from the Browser

Once you click on "View Results" the Self-Paced results window will open.

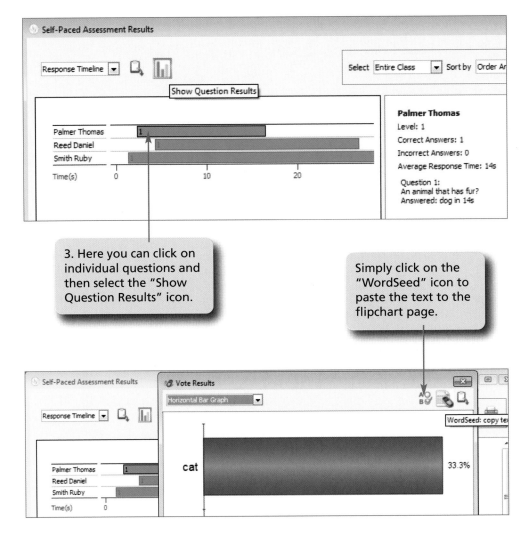

3. Here you can click on individual questions and then select the "Show Question Results" icon.

Simply click on the "WordSeed" icon to paste the text to the flipchart page.

If you have a number of questions, just select Q2 and repeat, then Q3 and so on. This facility allows students who are quick at texting (or thinking) to send in more than one idea in a texting activity.

Using groups with Self-Paced

When using ActivExpression in Self-Paced mode, you can create groups of students to work collaboratively. If you choose, you can also allocate a spokesperson for each individual group. Before following these instructions, ensure that all students are registered in named mode.

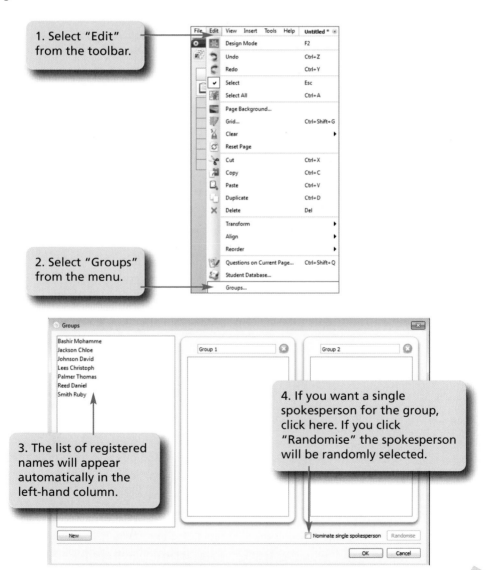

1. Select "Edit" from the toolbar.

2. Select "Groups" from the menu.

3. The list of registered names will appear automatically in the left-hand column.

4. If you want a single spokesperson for the group, click here. If you click "Randomise" the spokesperson will be randomly selected.

Using Groups with Self-Paced

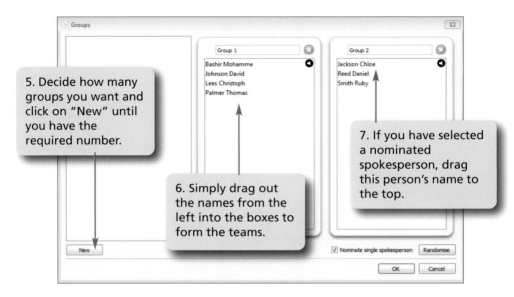

5. Decide how many groups you want and click on "New" until you have the required number.

6. Simply drag out the names from the left into the boxes to form the teams.

7. If you have selected a nominated spokesperson, drag this person's name to the top.

In this example with a nominated spokesperson, only Mohammed's and Chloe's handsets will receive a question and allow a response.

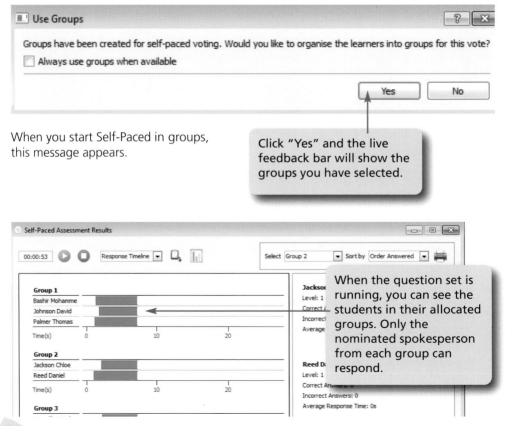

When you start Self-Paced in groups, this message appears.

Click "Yes" and the live feedback bar will show the groups you have selected.

When the question set is running, you can see the students in their allocated groups. Only the nominated spokesperson from each group can respond.

The Response Revolution

The Future

ActivExpression will not only improve the quality of learning but might also reduce costs. Few studies of the cost of photocopying are available, but most schools face huge bills for copying, especially in those schools where worksheets are the norm. Many substitute teachers survive on a diet of worksheets and with countless other teachers using them, many thousands of dollars/pounds are wasted each year in both the USA and the UK on copying, much of it on consumables. Question sets in ActivExpression can be used many times over and the marking, assessment, and analysis are done for the teacher—saving on their time as well. In the second edition of this book, a full evaluation of costs will be undertaken, but there is no doubt that in schools that have already invested in ActivExpression, the capital costs have been repaid in savings elsewhere.

ActivExpression creates an interactive, dynamic experience, giving all students the opportunity to engage in classroom discussions and take an active role in their learning. It allows teachers to use students' responses, combined with other student data, to gauge classroom comprehension and tailor instruction in "real time" to keep students on track. By combining the power of ActivExpression and ActivProgress, students, parents, teachers, and administrators are able to openly communicate and collaborate on learning outcomes and provide an even more powerful learning experience. Studies show that engaged learners are more apt to retain lessons and transfer these skills, and as a result are more prepared for the outside world. This powerful combination provides teachers with the essential tools to manage the classroom, assess students, and encourage collaboration.

The development of *ActivProgress* enables the results of assessments to be accumulated and analyzed in a variety of ways. Linking with existing school information systems, data can be used to make comparisons of students between classes, schools, or districts and this can be done over time, providing rich longitudinal data on progress. It also enables educators to incorporate other data on students so that a picture of the "whole child" can be developed.

Some schools and districts are successfully using ActivProgress and as the results of continuous assessments are accumulated, they will be able to reduce their reliance on summative, high-stakes testing. Such testing is very costly and many studies have shown how it can have negative side-effects such as "teaching to the test." ActivProgress offers data-mining and reporting functions that will make data immediate and useful. Over the period of a year, students might answer 20,000 questions—starters, main tasks, end-of-lesson assessments, formative and summative tests—and ActivProgress will manage that data and make it worth collecting for both analysis and intervention.

Using Smartphones, Pads and Computers

This year will see the launch of ActivEngage mobile. This software will run on all iOS4 devices (iPod touches, iPads, and iPhones) and all Android devices. Further developments will most likely include other Smartphones as demand requires. This means that in the future the students' own devices could be used for a variety of assessment purposes. Several schools in the USA are currently running BYOT (Bring Your Own Technology) pilots. These mobile devices will work seamlessly alongside existing ActivExpression handsets and ActivInspire.

ActivExpression handsets

A new handset will be launched later in 2011 that has a full QWERTY keyboard, a backlight, the ability to view and input equations in a natural format, and a set of symbols such as accents for use in foreign languages.

Self-Paced developments

The Self-Paced mode in ActivExpression is already a stunning development, but functions will continue to be added, including these that will appear in the coming months:

- Faced with a set of questions, students will be able to navigate around them like in a paper test, doing questions in the order of their choice.
- Teachers will be able to select an option for the "live feedback" to highlight the questions that are causing particular problems to students.

Finally, a message to all readers!

A second edition of this book will be published shortly and it will contain new sections. One will be on the use of ActivExpression and Self-Paced in surveys of student, parent, or community opinions, including an example which received glowing reports from inspectors in England. Another will be on their use in field work, and on school trips to museums, and so on. If you have examples like this, please send them to the publishers.

This book has many contributions from practicing teachers who have kindly shared their inspiration with readers. The second edition will do the same, and the publishers would be delighted to receive further examples of innovative practice. All contributions used will be acknowledged and copies of the book provided free of charge to the authors.

Send your intention to contribute to info@robertpowellpublications.com and the publishers will send you the necessary templates. Thank you in anticipation.

Join the Response Revolution

Our new website to share ideas and inspiration

www.theresponserevolution.com

Robert Powell Publications

Another book from Robert Powell

Robert Powell, the author of this book, is widely respected in the UK for his work with schools in improving the quality of teaching, learning, and assessment. He has led training sessions with over 500 Junior and High schools, and is renowned as a challenging and humorous speaker.

His handbook, based on the training sessions, is now into its third print, is widely used in the UK, and helps schools to promote outstanding teaching and learning anywhere in the world.

"This handbook is brilliant, combining a planning framework for leaders with a host of practical strategies for staff."

Mark Stanyer, Principal, Sir Stanley Matthews Academy

"The feedback from staff was immensely positive, with a number describing it as 'inspirational' and 'the best training session I have ever had'."

John Hartley, Headteacher, Saffron Walden High School

The book contains chapters on a wide range of strategies for:

- differentiation in planning tasks
- motivating and engaging students
- ground rules and classroom management
- building language skills
- participation in whole-class teaching
- assessment for learning

It also gives a set of principles for teaching, learning, and assessment. It shows how school leaders can develop a school ethos based on the principles while encouraging diversity and creativity within the classroom; consistency rather than conformity being the key.

To enquire about a speaking or training engagement for Robert Powell
email info@robertpowellpublications.com

Blockbusters

Blockbusters is a word game that was popular on TV in the UK for many years, and it proved an instant hit when adapted for education, teaching the key words of subjects like Science.

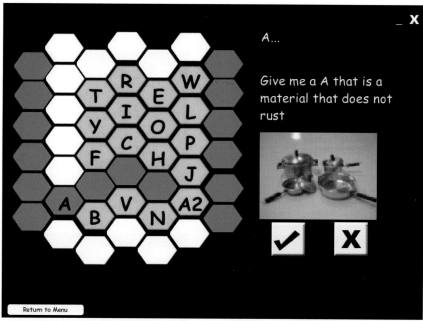

The Blockbusters games are based on the Thames Television program BLOCKBUSTERS.
Licensed by FremantleMedia Enterprises. www.fremantlemedia.com.
The Blockbusters music written by Ed Welch, published by EMI Music Publishing Ltd.

Played in two teams, Blue and White, the first team to connect left to right (Blue) or top to bottom (White) wins. Each letter is the first letter of a key word. The children learn the words very quickly!

The Editor, which comes with the software, allows users to create their own games with text, images, or sound clues. It is ideal for building vocabulary in a foreign language since learners can get sound clues, spoken clues, or reading clues to guess the words.

Titles suitable for the USA: Science, Physical Education, French, Spanish, and German. Other subjects are available for the UK.

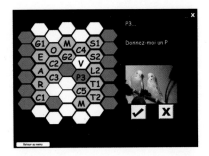

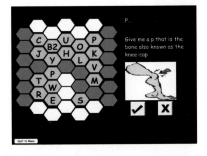

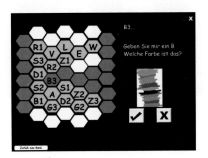

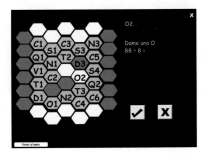

See the Blockbusters games in action at www.robertpowellpublications.com